Great Houses *of*
FLORIDA

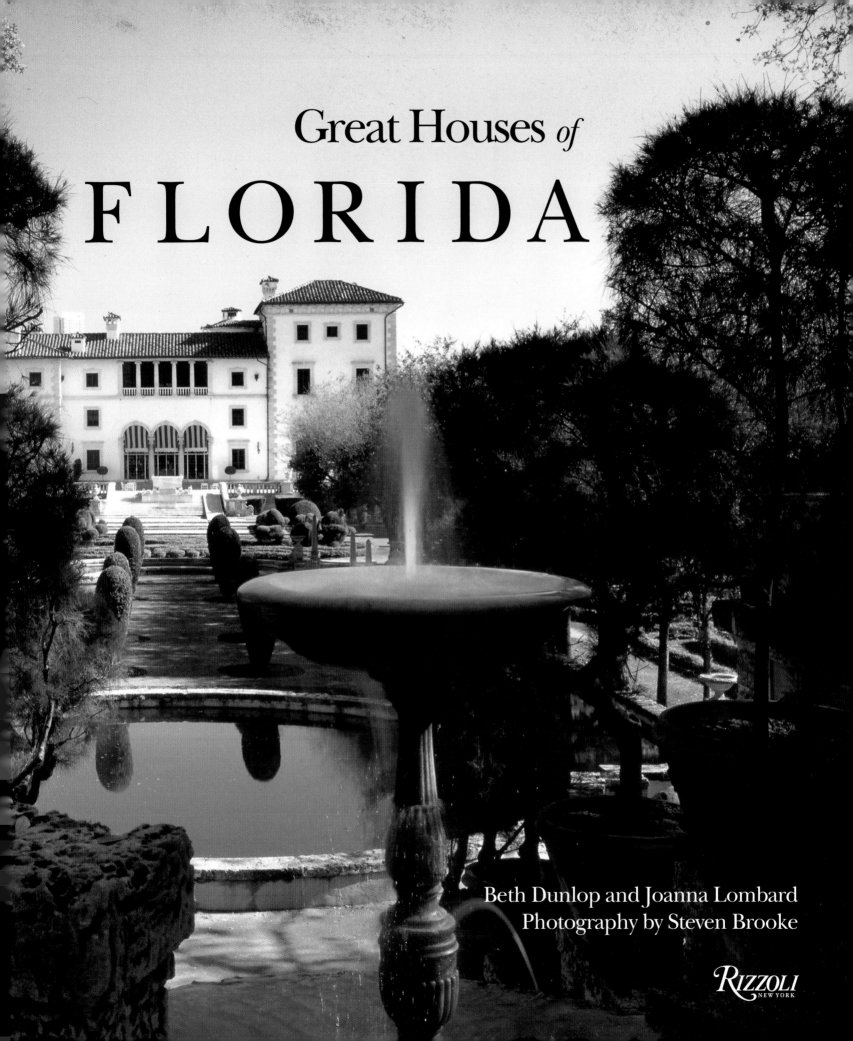

Great Houses of
FLORIDA

Beth Dunlop and Joanna Lombard
Photography by Steven Brooke

RIZZOLI
NEW YORK

To my parents, who first showed me Florida.
To Scott, Robin, Heather, and Alison
for experiencing it with me back when.
And, as always, to Bill and Adam
for joining me as we found it again. — **BD**

To my mother and father — **JL**

To Suzanne and Miles — **SB**

First published in the United States of America in 2008
by Rizzoli International Publications, Inc.
300 Park Avenue South
New York, NY 10010
www.rizzoliusa.com

ISBN-13: 978-0-8478-3097-8
Library of Congress Catalog Control Number:
2008922993

2008 2009 2010 2011 / 10 9 8 7 6 5 4 3 2 1

Distributed in the U.S. by Random House, New York

Printed in China

Editor, Philip A. Reeser
Designer, Abigail Sturges

HALF-TITLE PAGE
*Detail of entrance doors of El Jardin, John Bindley's
1918 Miami residence.*

TITLE PAGE
*View overlooking the gardens toward the southern
facade of Vizcaya, James Deering's 1916 Miami villa.*

Contents

Preface

The authors gratefully acknowledge the dedication of the people of Florida who, through the Department of Historic Resources and the Florida Park System, support and advance preservation throughout the state. Because of the efforts of numerous individuals and groups, and with the leadership and financial assistance provided by the professional staff in the state, many of the houses in this book are open to the public today.

This book presents a limited number of houses, chosen first because they are open to the public and second because they continue to exert a powerful influence on the iconography and architecture of Florida today. The indefatigable and brilliant photographer Steven Brooke, along with our astute and diligent editors at Rizzoli, David Morton, Douglas Curran, and Philip Reeser, and the always-inspired Abigail Sturges, who designed *Great Houses of Florida* with such virtuosity, bring this project to life.

As the work of writers coming from different points of view, one a full-time writer, editor, and architecture journalist, the other a faculty member and practicing architect—the book also represents a newly defined common ground that attempts to present the houses directly, with related research available for the inquisitive reader. In this effort, we appreciate the support of our colleagues who offered insight and advice regarding the crucial houses to include. Dean Elizabeth Plater-Zyberk of the University of Miami School of Architecture, in particular, offered important material assistance to the project.

The preservationists, curators, archivists, and volunteers who operate these houses represent an incredible group of inspired and accomplished advocates. They provided both their guidance and time, as well as access to the houses and historic materials. The book would not exist without them and although listed here in gratitude, they are not responsible for errors or omissions.

Last, the authors thank all our family members who patiently set aside days, nights, weekends, and numerous events in order to make time for the houses. Having lived with the constant presence of the owners, builders, and occupants of these houses for the last twenty months, they are as eager as we to see this book in print and occupying the minds and hearts of the many friends and visitors for whom Florida is still the fascinating and ever-changing landscape of dream and reality.

OPPOSITE
Entrance arches leading to front door of Casa Feliz, the 1932 Winter Park residence of Robert Bruce Barbour.

Introduction

Joanna Lombard and Beth Dunlop

In Florida, time is a wheel. Although the houses age, more or less gracefully, each generation relives Florida's story. It is a freshly recurring scenario formed long ago by the embrace of promoters and investors whose efforts produced cycles of profits—sometimes in wild excess—followed by bouts of despair. "It was a simple pitch," wrote Christine Haughney and Vikas Bajaj in the *New York Times* in February 2007. "Investors would put little to no money down and take out construction loans that a developer would use to build modest homes in a fast-growing stretch of Southwest Florida." Unfortunately, the 482 investors in this project ended up "with half-built houses and thousands of dollars in construction liens."[1]

The *New York Times* featured the same story eighty years earlier, explaining that, although Florida's real estate "was reputed to have made thousands fabulously rich overnight and to have caused cities to rise almost by magic from reclaimed swamplands or barren wastes of sand," the current reality of the 1927 new year was not the newly minted millionaire. Instead, "hundreds of persons who bought property during the boom and made an initial payment of 20 or 25 percent in cash were unwilling to make further payments when the slump came and chose rather to write off their deficits and let the investment drop."[2] Thus, Florida's history is not necessarily a tale of times past; it lives on, repeating itself in the present day, both illuminating and shading contemporary conditions. It is through this lens that we look at Florida's historic houses.

The foundation of the story is Florida's land, or, more accurately, the lack of it. Travel on Florida's roads, and the landscape looks solid. Fly above, and solidity gives way to the aqueous base that is Florida's reality, making its land the object of lust, greed, and envy, as well as admiration, appreciation, and reverence. Water dominates—from the Florida Bay, between the Atlantic Ocean and the Gulf of Mexico, laced through the Everglades to Lake

Okeechobee, to the headwaters of the north-flowing St. Johns River and the Lake District. Maps from as early as 1830, produced by the United States Army Corps of Engineers to guide troops in the war against the Seminoles, offer an understanding of this. On these maps, the center of Florida, and most of its southern peninsula, is a landscape of nearly inaccessible islands dotting broad glades of water.

The northern section of the Everglades once extended from the eastern coastal ridge to the western flood plains. Fed by the system of lakes and rivers that spilled through Lake Okeechobee, the watery plains formed a vast liquid center surrounded by the skeletal fingers of the peninsula. For most of the last century and a half the promise held by the thin ridgeline of the coast and the fertile ground of the Lake District inspired myriad schemes to drain the Everglades in order to create agriculturally productive land. Today, the southeast coast has climbed over its ridge to spread across the plains, while the southwest coast has expanded toward the middle. Lake Okeechobee is severed from its natural reception and dispersal of river water to the glades, and development has spread throughout the Lake District. The vastly reduced acreage of the Everglades is a result of millions of dollars and decades of determined interests seeking farmland, access, and housing, with varying degrees of success.

In this context, patterns of settlement emerge gradually, first in the Spanish encampments of St. Augustine and Pensacola, then in the sailing ports. St. Augustine's shallow water formed a strong defensive barrier but limited its capacity as a port; shipping lanes favored Apalachicola, Jacksonville, Key West, and Tampa. Apalachicola bustled with cotton exports, especially in the years before the Civil War, and, in later decades, timber. Through most of the nineteenth century, the approach to Florida other than by water was limited to the intrepid explorer. Even the most enthusiastic tourists ventured only as far as

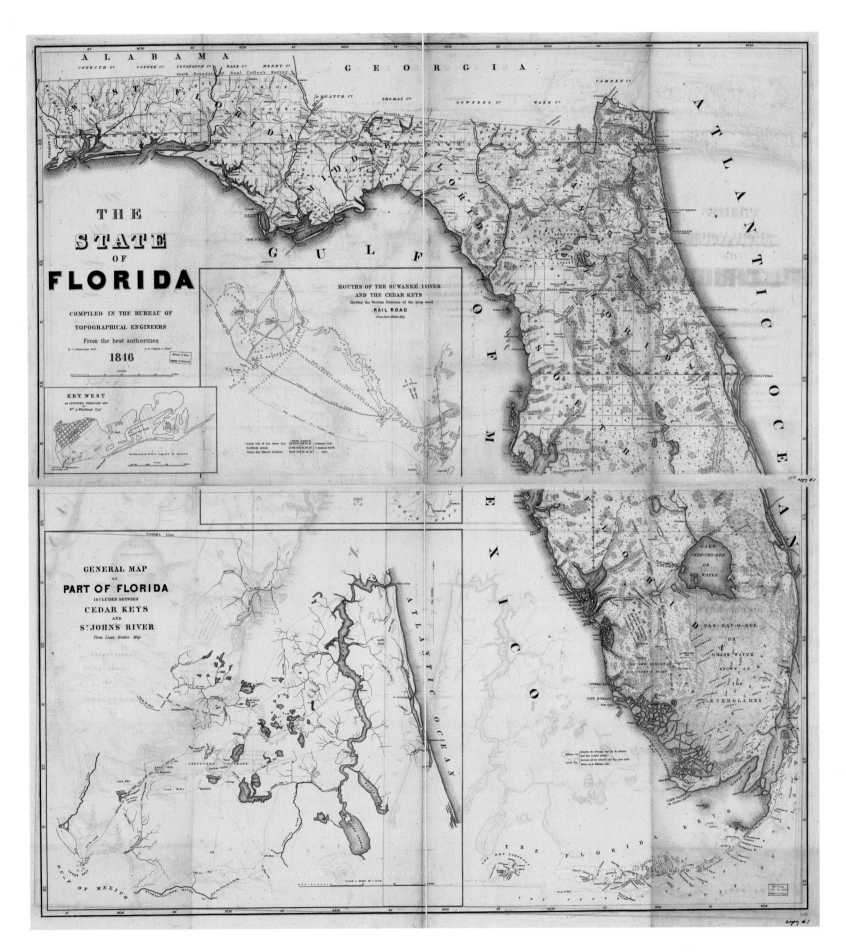

THE
STATE
OF
FLORIDA

COMPILED IN THE BUREAU OF
TOPOGRAPHICAL ENGINEERS
From the best authorities
1846

KEY WEST

MOUTHS OF THE SUWANEÉ RIVER
AND THE CEDAR KEYS
Shewing the Western Terminus of the proposed
RAIL ROAD

GENERAL MAP
OF
PART OF FLORIDA
INCLUDED BETWEEN
CEDAR KEYS
AND
St JOHN'S RIVER

the steamboats would go, along the banks of the St. Johns River and then across Daytona to the Atlantic Ocean for travel to Key West, Havana, or Nassau.

It was not until the 1880s that Henry Flagler and Henry Plant reassembled Florida's twenty-year-old railroads and laid new lines that would begin to fully open the state. Flagler's railroad headed south along the eastern coast, first to St. Augustine, then Daytona and Ormond Beach, onward to Palm Beach, reaching Miami in 1896, and finally to Key West on January 22, 1912.[3] Meanwhile, Plant collected the traffic across the state to Tampa and its access to global ports. In those early years, though, Florida was neither easy to traverse nor comfortable to inhabit. Even Mary Barr Munroe—wife of author Kirk Munroe and noted Coconut Grove hostess—ever the optimist, acknowledged the trials of Florida's pioneer life. Writing in her journal on May 21, 1896, she declared "the main drawback in Miami at present is the rocks—rocks in the streets, rocks on the sidewalks, rocks everywhere." She understood that the curious rocks were, in fact, the oolitic limestone that forms the geologic foundation of the region and the source of Miami's water, but still she felt that the rocks made the water "bad, both for drinking and washing."

Even more distressing to her were "the mail facilities" which she described as "execrable, being but three times a week when it is at its best." Worse, she knew that the overland and river passages could "sometimes take a letter a week to go from West Palm Beach to Miami, and sometimes it never gets there." Indefatigable though, Munroe summons her faith that all will be "changed. The rocks will be removed, good water secured, and ample mail facilities provided."[4] Her positive spirit indicates the powerful allure of this exotic place and she is confident that the future will be better.

The notion of better depended on the prognosticator, though. To the professional and amateur botanists and naturalists who were drawn to the state, initially in the north and by the end of the nineteenth century to the south, the flora and fauna were paradisiacal. Aside from the tropical storms, and even those were thought to have ecological purpose as seeds and plants from the islands were carried to the peninsula and the tangled tropical growth endured a massive trim, Florida offered ground for productive plant experimentation.

Orange groves, initially established near DeLand, gradually moved away from the frost to the south and east (to the coastal land warmed by the Gulf Stream and the balmy ocean breezes), while much farther south, David Fairchild, having introduced tropical plants to the nation, delighted in the opportunity to test his findings on his own plot of land at the Kampong. He advised Charles Deering, who provided the land for the state's first plant

introduction station at his Buena Vista estate, and helped Fairchild relocate the station to the south when development chased them down the coast. Charles Deering then rescued and preserved acres of hammock and pineland on what became his Cutler Estate, while sponsoring the travel, study, and publications of John Kunkel Small, the taxonomist and botanical explorer who was head curator of the New York Botanical Garden. Small also advised

Thomas A. Edison in his quest for rubber-producing plants, an effort that motivated the construction of Edison's lab in Fort Myers and united Edison with Harvey Firestone as well as Henry Ford, who built his own winter home next door to Edison's. Small's travels through Florida inspired his call to Floridians to stop the rampant destruction of the natural resources of the state. Published with Deering's support, *From Eden to Sahara,*

Florida's Tragedy showed photographs of areas Small visited in 1910 contrasted with the same locations in the 1920s. Small hoped this evidence of the rapidly disappearing mangroves and hammocks would inspire greater respect for Florida's landscape. What actually ensured the preservation of various parts of the state was the cycle of "boom and bust," eras in which development flourished followed by periods of recession, if not depression—a

*The early eighteenth-
century Gonzalez-Alvarez
House in St. Augustine
is the oldest surviving
house from the city's
Spanish Colonial
period.*

cycle that recurs even in the postmillennial era. The periods of quiet allowed natural resources to flourish and permitted threatened architecture to remain standing.

Most of Florida's earliest houses succumbed to climate and age, although some methods of building
assured perpetuity. The first Spanish settlers of the six-
teenth century followed the example of the native Timu-
cuans and built with thatch and board extracted from a
vast forest of oak, pine, and palmetto. The buildings that
are now most emblematic of St. Augustine came much
later. The Spaniards, seeking a fireproof method of building for the powder magazine, developed "tabby," a lime-
and-sand mixture with an oyster-shell aggregate. Shell-
stone, which the Spanish called *coquina*, and stucco followed. After the successful use of masonry construction in
1596 in the powder magazine of the fort, civic buildings
were built of tabby, stone, and stucco and finally by 1746,
the majority of St. Augustine's domestic buildings were
tabby and coquina construction.[5]

While St. Augustine and Pensacola were the largest
towns, in February 1739 Spanish governor Montiano also
established the first free-black community in North America just north of St. Augustine, Gracia Real de Santa
Teresa de Mosé, known as Fort Mose. Many of its citizens
evacuated to Cuba when the English acquired Florida in
1763. When Spain reestablished control in Florida by
1784, new communities were established. By the time that
Spain relinquished Florida to the United States in 1821,
shiploads of Spanish colonists, along with "Yamasees from
St. Augustine and five Apalaches," sailed to Hispaniola,
leaving Florida to its journey with the confederacy.
Although free-black communities survived this transition,
Daniel Schafer argues that while not benevolent, Spanish
rule permitted a more "flexible system of race relations."

The Americans, he feels, presented a highly dogmatic
authority that viewed the free-black communities as
"threatening contradictions to pro-slavery theory and
incendiary inspirations for slave insurrections."[6] Along
with the human and social tragedies wreaked by these
new policies, a further result, parallel to the war conducted on the Seminoles, limited the survival of the architecture of these groups. It is nearly impossible for
persecuted and war-torn populations to develop an architectural and urban legacy.

What evidence remains today is, therefore, in need
of attention and preservation, if not reconstruction.
Although not among the sites currently operating as visitor centers and museums with predictable schedules and
steady staff, this aspect of Florida's history merits significant investigation.

The occupying government not only influenced the
materials, but also the pattern of building. The townscape
of St. Augustine and the very brief French settlement at
Fort Caroline were followed by the lengthier British occupation of East and West Florida, yielding a rural pattern
of county seats organized around rice and indigo plantations. Unlike the haunting loss of the intact towns of the
freed black and Native-American communities, the Spanish eras imprinted a vague connection to a Mediterranean
dream that would once again capture the nation's imagination in the early twentieth century and become the
style of building most closely associated with Florida.[7]

The actual Spanish influence can still be seen in
small clusters of houses in St. Augustine, Pensacola, and
Tampa's Ybor City. Each "village" tells a different story
from a different era, from the homes of the Spanish
"occupiers" in St. Augustine to the grander and more settled residences of prosperous nineteenth-century Pensacola to the no less architecturally significant workers'
houses built for the Cuban immigrant cigar makers in
Tampa. Each of these tells a story of a specific time and
place. Elsewhere—as can be seen in the home of Marjorie
Kinnan Rawlings, the author who brought the hardscrab-
ble Central Florida landscape and life to national attention in such books as her Pulitzer Prize-winning novel,
The Yearling (1938)—spareness and simplicity ruled. If
Victoriana had found fertile ground along the banks of
the St. Johns River and in the houses of DeLand, pragma-
tism and the regional necessities of dealing with a climate
that was often severely hot helped shape the rural residences of Florida.

But by the late nineteenth and into the early twentieth century, an international language of architecture
began to take hold of the houses of Florida, starting in
1888 with the hotels commissioned by Henry Flagler in
St. Augustine. There he asked the then-fledgling firm of
Carrère & Hastings to create two hotels, which they did—

after a trip to Spain—in a fashion that was evocative of a panoply of Spanish influences. The buildings set the stage for decades of Florida architecture. The architectural historian Michael McDonough attributes the subsequent interest in the Mediterranean style to the influences of San Diego's 1915 Panama-California Exposition and "A Street in Cairo" exhibition at the 1893 World's Columbian Exposition in Chicago, as well as the proliferation of similarly themed amusement-park buildings, and the desire to inhabit the fantastic movie sets of *Blood and Sand* (1922) and *Don Q, Son of Zorro* (1925).[8]

But always within the larger stream of shared aesthetic interests, focused individualists—the yachtsman Ralph Munroe, who built his house like his ships, closely calibrated to provide shade and enhance airflow, the artist Frederic Bartlett, who experimented with native materials to produce a new tropical prototype—established independent forms of expression. More modestly, yet no less significantly, writers such as Marjorie Kinnan Rawlings at Cross Creek and Ernest Hemingway in Key West inhabited houses that offered respite. And each subsequent generation looked toward transitional spaces to calibrate the climate to a tolerable level of comfort. Whether humble porches or grand galleries, the transitional spaces that were roofed but open-air, cooled the blanket of air closest to the interior rooms, for the smallest cottages and the largest villas.

The combination of vernacular traditions and architectural intent continued to intertwine the great estates and smaller dwellings. James Deering traveled the Brenta River in Italy to discover the model for Vizcaya, his 130-acre estate that would host its own farm, railroad stop, and enough property and staff to sustain life and accommodate festivities.[9] Attracted to the exoticism of the native plants, Deering reserved a small portion—the ten acres of Vizcaya gardens open to the public today—as a formal garden, and dedicated 117 acres of the designed landscape to traversing the mangrove and hammocks with canals and pathways, engaging the visitor in the tangled spectacle of mangroves edging the vastness of Biscayne Bay.

As the craftsmen of Vizcaya moved south to begin work on El Jardin, the architect Richard Kiehnel later commented that both Vizcaya and El Jardin enjoyed "the distinction of having given the impetus to the construction in southern Florida of homes of the style which we now know as Mediterranean." Kiehnel, writing ten years later, explains that in southern Florida in 1916, the two estates "were the only examples of the architecture of Southern Italy and Spain which were to be found here," noting that "the beautiful residences now adorning Miami Beach and the numbers of Mediterranean homes now to be found in Coral Gables, at that time were scarcely thought of."[10]

Some of the grandest houses, such as Flagler's Whitehall in Palm Beach, remained distinct from the trend, perhaps because the Carrère & Hastings language had not yet found a tropical variation; if their Ponce de León and Alcazar hotels in St. Augustine had launched the proverbial "thousand ships" of architecture in the Spanish-Mediterranean style, Whitehall established the neoclassical, a less profusely emulated style. This grew ever more to be the case as Palm Beach evolved early in the twentieth century with the Hispano-Moresque architecture of Addison Mizner, whose great Palm Beach houses even today (nary a single one is in public hands or open to visitors) set a standard for the very rich. Mizner, of course, was followed by the Swiss-born Maurice Fatio, whose work (likewise all still in private ownership) exemplifies the era. Mar-a-Lago, designed by Joseph Urban and completed in 1927, is—among all the Palm Beach houses of what might be called the "Mizner era"—the only one to offer even partial public access.[11] Urban conceived this house, which he designed for Marjorie Merriweather Post (she was then married to Edward F. Hutton), as a Moorish palace, though in the typical fashion of Florida Gilded-Age houses, it bows more to the idea of the Moresque than to the reality.

It is only when architectural ambition coincides with both popular taste and local materials that the influence of a building seems able to extend outward to inspire a vernacular tradition of its own. Thus, Whitehall remains less imitated, while Mar-a-Lago in Palm Beach or John and Mable Ringling's Cà d'Zan continues to inspire homes and buildings across the region. The Mediterranean style of architecture—that particular melding of

styles from across southern Europe and North Africa—reached its fullest expression, perhaps, in the development of the city of Coral Gables. There, a style once exclusive to the very rich was made egalitarian and utopian. It was found in both "palaces," if that is what such hotels as the Coral Gables Biltmore implied, and tiny cottages, which the advertising slogans of the time referred to as "Everyman's Castle."

Understanding the intricate relationship between landmark architecture and vernacular buildings in revealing both tradition and history, the state of Florida has championed preservation across the spectrum of houses that range from grand estates to one-room dwellings. Through its division of historical resources, as well as the Florida state parks, the state government has been a vital partner to towns, cities, and counties, supporting projects that encompass extensive acreage, as well as small collections held in individual rooms. This advocacy has nurtured local, historical, and preservation societies that have initiated dramatic rescues of the history that remains.

Even in places where the past is barely evident, a focus on history is emerging as an important force. In Fort Lauderdale, for example, where most of the historic downtown succumbed to a bulldozing frenzy in the late

ABOVE
Whitehall—the winter residence of Henry Flagler and his wife, Mary Lily Kenan Flagler—brought the Gilded Age to Palm Beach in Carrere & Hastings's design for the 55-room, 60,000-square-foot structure. Courtesy of the Library of Congress.

RIGHT
Built in 1888 by Henry Flagler with architecture by Carrère & Hastings, and interiors planned by Louis Comfort Tiffany, the former Ponce de León Hotel is a masterpiece of Spanish Renaissance architecture and is listed on the National Register of Historic Places. The building in St. Augustine is now a residence hall at Flagler College.

1960s, the Stranahan House perseveres with a staunch group of supporters who value the last historic downtown house still standing in its original location. Among the cities whose prosperity declined when steamboat lines ceased or when interstate travel displaced local highways and rail lines, many of the historic downtowns are still intact. Having escaped the destruction of a building boom, these buildings are the core of downtown restoration efforts. DeLand, for example, brings the era of the steamboat suburb to life, nourished by active preservationists, an engaged university, and many significant historic houses.

The power of the historic houses of Florida as sentinels of the past and guideposts to the future is already attracting public interest in the broader cultural landscape, which includes both designed and natural landscape, and energizing the movement to restore wetlands and rivers, and develop greener and more sustainable communities. While Florida's history is filled with dastardly deeds and heroic adventures, almost all of which involve a transformation or restoration of a natural condition, the stewards of the present seek a more benevolent outcome. The historic houses of Florida offer insight and prominently bear witness to the past; they also illuminate the possibilities of the future.

NOTES

1. Christine Haughney and Vikas Bajaj, "Lofty Hopes, Suspended," *New York Times*, February 22, 2007.
2. "Florida Is Facing Serious Reaction," *New York Times* (1857–current file); Jan 3, 1927; ProQuest Historical Newspapers, *New York Times* (1851–2003), p. 3.
3. Les Standiford, *Last Train to Paradise: Henry Flagler and the Spectacular Rise and Fall of the Railroad That Crossed an Ocean*, New York: Crown Publishers, 2002: 201.
4. Marr Barr Munroe in *Miami Diary 1896: A Day by Day Account of Events That Occurred the Year Miami Became a City*, Ann Spach Chesney, France G. Hunter, Harriet Stiger Liles, Ann Josberger McFadden, Eliza Phillips Ruden, and Larry Wiggins, Miami: Miami Centennial, 1996: 73.
5. Albert Manucy, *The Houses of St. Augustine*, St. Augustine: The St. Augustine Historical Society, [1962] 1978:14-33.
6. Daniel L. Schafer, "A Class of People Neither Freemen Nor Slaves": From Spanish to American Race Relations in Florida, 1821-1861, *Journal of Social History*, Vol. 26, no. 3 (Spring, 1993): 587.
7. Robert L. Gold, "The Settlement of the Pensacola Indians in New Spain, 1763–1770," *The Hispanic American Historical Review*, Vol. 45, no. 4., November 1965: 567-8.
8. Michael McDonough, "Selling Sarasota: Architecture and Propaganda in a 1920s Boom Town," in *The Journal of Decorative and Propaganda Arts*: Volume 23, 1998:15–17.
9. James Maher, *The Twilight of Splendor: Chronicles of the Age of American Palaces*, New York: Little Brown & Company, 1975:164.
10. Richard Kiehnel, "El Jardin," *Tropical Home and Garden*, Vol. I, No. 4, August 1928:5.
11. It is now a private club under the ownership of Donald Trump and open to its members and guests, as well as occasional parties.

LEFT
Completed in January of 1927, the Mar-a-Lago estate in Palm Beach was designed by the versatile Viennese architect Joseph Urban for Marjorie Merriweather Post (then Mrs. E.F. Hutton). Courtesy of the Library of Congress.

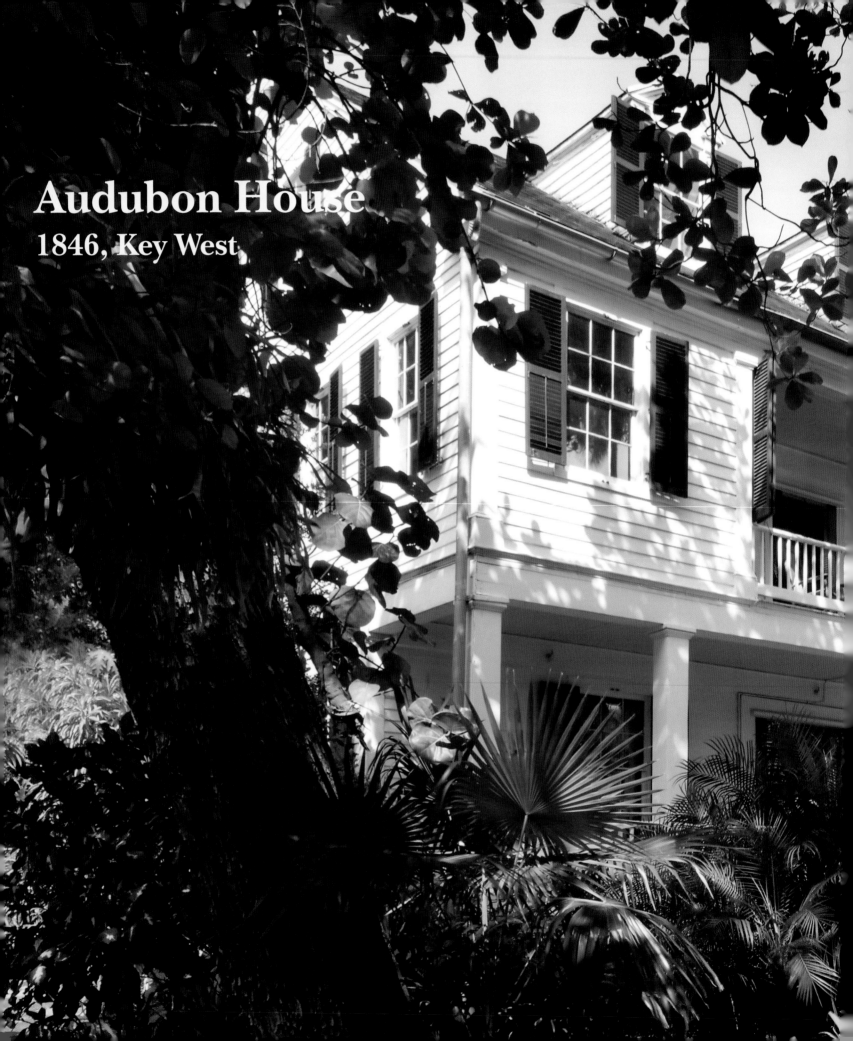

Audubon House

1846, Key West

John James Audubon never lived in Audubon House, but in 1832 he lingered in what would become the gardens there. During his stay in Key West, he discovered eighteen new birds that live on in his exquisite folio drawings, many of which may have been created in the gardens of the gabled, wooden house on Whitehead Street.

Not long after that, Captain John H. Geiger moved to Key West, and in 1846, built a three-story house for his family. A skilled ship's captain and wrecker, Geiger accrued a fortune from the vessels that capsized in the offshore reefs; from court cases alone, he is known to have salvaged fifty-seven ships. Geiger became Key West's first harbor pilot. Geiger lived here with his wife and nine children, and the house remained in family hands for more than a century.

The house features a broad central hall and staircase. Rooms open onto either side of the hall, allowing for the flow of air throughout. Among Geiger's innovations were half shutters that line the verandas on the second floor; the shutters kept rain out, but let air in.

PREVIOUS PAGES
The Audubon House was built in 1846 by Captain John H. Geiger. Today it is named after John James Audubon, commemorating his 1832 expedition to the Florida Keys.

LEFT
The parlor was the social center of the home. Here, the Geiger family gathered around a central table, like this one in mahogany, where they sewed, listened to music, or played cards.

19

FAR LEFT
The separate dining room in the Audubon House was a luxury afforded by few nineteenth-century Key West families. The room, typical of early- and mid-nineteenth-century American custom, was a multifunctional room used during the day for tea, sewing, or reading.

LEFT
The master bedroom used by John and Lucretia Geiger shows the mosquito netting that many early Key West residents used to shelter themselves from the mosquitoes that plagued them with disease.

By 1958, however, the house had fallen into disrepair and was slated for demolition when the Wolfson family intervened. Pioneers in their own right, the Wolfsons arrived in Key West in 1884 and ultimately developed an important presence there; the Mitchell Wolfson Family Foundation's purchase of the Geiger House (and its subsequent transformation into the Audubon House) is considered to be the starting point of Key West's historic preservation movement.

The board-and-batten house with its prominent rooftop dormer windows and first- and second-story porches has been carefully restored. The Wolfson Family Foundation has sought antiques that would have been typical of the home of a wealthy nineteenth-century family. Over the years, the foundation has acquired twenty-eight Audubon first editions, which are also on display in the house.

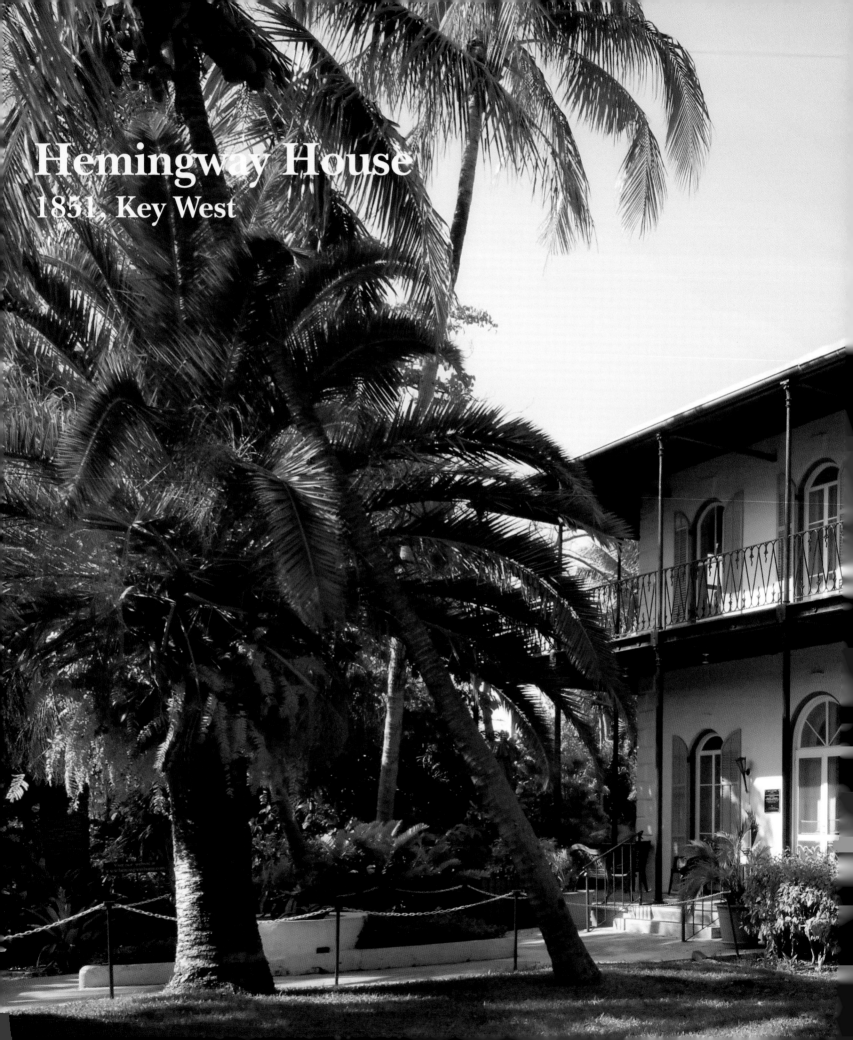

Hemingway House
1851, Key West

I t was in Key West that Ernest Hemingway completed his novel, *A Farewell to Arms*, and wrote *To Have and Have Not*. He also wrote two of his most famous short stories there, *The Snows of Kilimanjaro* and *The Short Happy Life of Francis Macomber*. The Hemingways had retreated to Key West from Paris, first renting and then moving into this two-story house on Whitehead Street.

The winner of both the Nobel and Pulitzer prizes, Hemingway was born in Oak Park, Illinois, in 1899, and at nineteen set off to serve with the Red Cross in World War I. He married Hadley Richardson, lived in Paris, and began writing—at first short stories and then the novel *The Sun Also Rises*. By 1927 he was divorced, and remarried to Pauline Pfeiffer. The following year the couple set sail for Key West via Havana.

The house they bought in Key West had been built in 1851 by a maritime architect and wrecker named Asa Tift. Using the coquina limestone found on the land, Tift built a solid, somewhat sober house with arched windows and porches that was set back from the street and surrounded by gardens. Ernest and Pauline Hemingway moved into the house in 1931, after Pauline's uncle, Gus

LEFT
The high arched windows of the house, as shown in the first-floor living room, provide ample light and views of the garden.

BELOW
Hemingway's typewriter.

OPPOSITE
The dining room features an eighteenth-century walnut table, chairs from Spain, and a Murano-glass chandelier. The walls are covered with family portraits.

Pfeiffer, purchased the house for them for $8,000. Pauline added bathrooms in the Art Deco style of the day and a pool, which—like so much else in this house—has become the stuff of lore. The pool was thought to be the subject of a famous spat between Ernest and Pauline, but many years later Hemingway's writer grandson John wrote about it this way: "The house is one of the few on the island with a basement and the first to have a swimming pool. Both the basement and the pool were carved out of solid limestone and if you take the tour they'll tell you that Ernest, on his way back from the Spanish Civil War, was so aghast at the money my grandmother spent digging out the pool that he threw what he called his 'last

LEFT
*The headboard of the
bed in the master
bedroom was originally
a gate from a Spanish
monastery. The
painting above the bed
is a more recent
acquisition as
Hemingway had a Joan
Miro painting in that
spot when he lived there.*

penny' into the still wet cement of the patio, which, while
dramatic, probably never happened. Ernest loved to swim
and used the pool to stay in shape, but like much of what
people think they know about Papa his 'last penny' has
more to do with the myth than the reality of his life."

Hemingway had a son, Jack, from his first marriage.
He and Pauline had two more children, Patrick and Gregory, who spent their childhoods in the Key West house,
though not all of it with their father. Hemingway's stay in
Key West was not to survive a decade; by 1936 he had met
Martha Gellhorn, who was to become his third wife, and
thus divorced Pauline, leaving her with a 51 percent ownership of the house. After Pauline's death in 1951, Hemingway returned to the house intermittently. By 1961 it
had fallen into some disrepair, and the property was sold
to Bernice Dickson, who opened the house to the public
in 1965.

ABOVE
*The "modern" bathroom
with its art-deco tile
flooring was installed by
Pauline Hemingway.*

FOLLOWING PAGES
*Typical of the era, the
Asa Tift house was built
with broad loggias to
help shade the interior
spaces.*

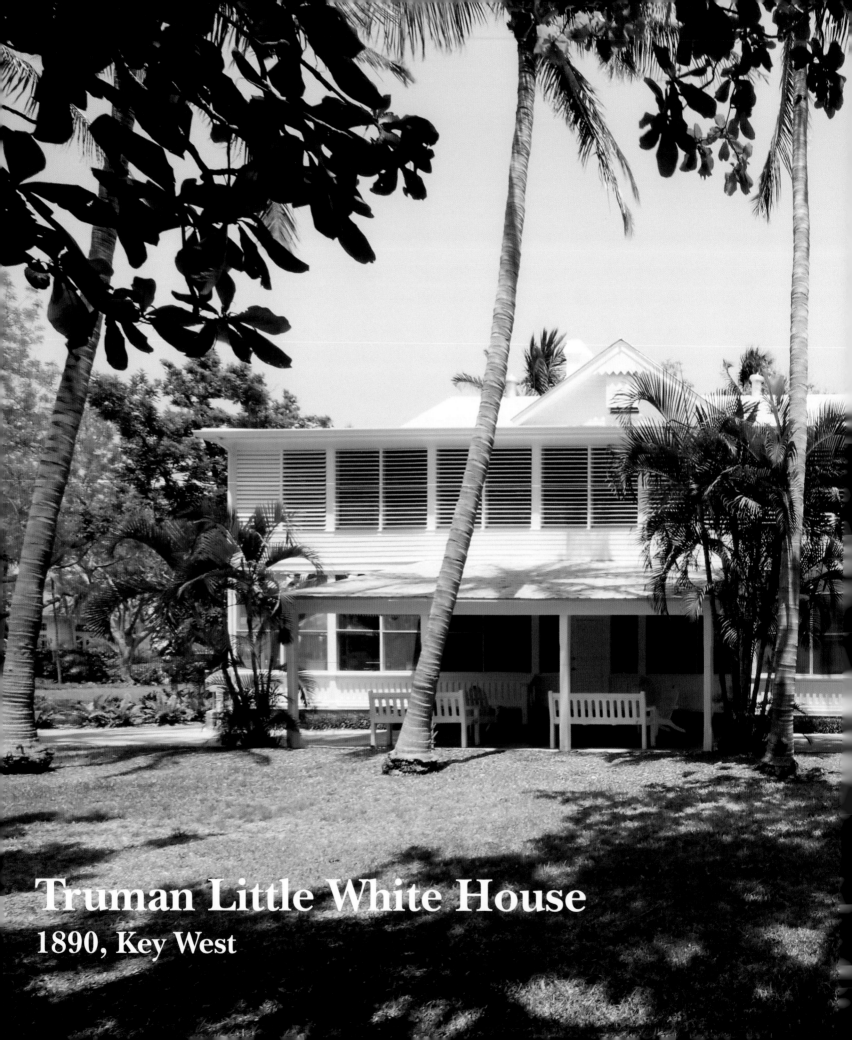

Truman Little White House
1890, Key West

PREVIOUS PAGES
The Truman Little White House with its double loggias was built at the end of the nineteenth century.

ABOVE
A November 1948 photograph shows President Harry S. Truman, flanked by his wife Bess and their daughter Margaret, on the lawn outside the Little White House. Courtesy of the State Archives of Florida.

RIGHT
The presidential desk where Truman wrote the letter that led to General Douglas MacArthur's resignation.

OPPOSITE
Bess Truman's sitting room as it was in 1949.

In 1877, Commander J. K. Winn of the United States Navy wrote to his superior officer to point out that Key West was the only military station where "quarters" were not provided. He informed him that officers stationed in Key West were forced to rent rooms in boarding houses that were "less than satisfactory."

Six years later as the United States began to ready itself for the Spanish-American War, two wood-frame buildings were constructed, the first for the base commandant and the second for the paymaster. Robert Wolz and Barbara Mayo recount that the architect, George McKay, specified "frame structures, two stories high, without cellars, and surrounded with piazzas on both first and second stories." The building—actually a "duplex" or basically two attached single-family homes—was called Quarters A and B and was begun in 1890.

The architecture reflected Key West's roots as a settling place for both Bahamian "Tories" (Loyalists who had fled the United States after the Revolution) and seafaring New Englanders, but—with its deep double loggias—it also embraced the house's semitropical setting. Shortly after the Key West harbor was dredged to allow for ever-larger ships, Quarters A and B were converted into a spacious single-family house for use by the commandant alone.

The house served as the Key West Naval Station's command center during the Spanish-American War as well as during World War I and World War II. In 1946, President Harry S. Truman made the first of what would be eleven trips to the Little White House. These visits are recorded in official presidential trip logs, which form the historical documentation of the time Truman spent in Key West. "The party soon shifted to lighter clothing as it was quite warm at Key West. Then after a casual inspection of their pleasant and spacious quarters, the president and his party settled down to spend the remainder of their day relaxing and resting after their five-hour plane ride from Washington," the first of these logs (November 17–23) reported. Much later, Truman's grandson, Clifton Truman Daniel, would write: "Grandpa especially liked to swim, often as a prelude to the napping, bourbon, and poker. Near the Little White House, the story goes, there was no natural beach, so engineers trucked in sand and dumped it where the land dropped off to the water. They added a little cabana where he could change into his trunks."

Those were history-changing times. While in residence at his Little White House, Truman worked on both the Marshall Plan and the Truman Doctrine as well as the

NEAR RIGHT
The office and living room.

FAR RIGHT
The dining room is almost entirely original. It was here that the Department of Defense was created in 1947 when then–General Eisenhower met with President Truman.

RIGHT
Truman's poker table, which can be converted to a dining table, was made in 1949 by civilian workers in the naval base cabinet shop; its ashtrays were made of three-inch shell casings.

recognition of the State of Israel. It was in Key West that he took some seminal steps, such as the fourth civil rights executive order, which required the hiring of minorities, and the two-week cease-fire in Korea, the act that caused General Douglas MacArthur to resign.

Later, Presidents Dwight D. Eisenhower and John F. Kennedy stayed in the Little White House, the former while recuperating from a heart attack and the latter when he met with British Prime Minister Harold Macmillan in 1961, just days before the Bay of Pigs invasion and then again in 1963 just after the Cuban missile crisis.

The naval base was renamed the Truman Annex in 1973, but only a year later the "annex" portion of the base closed, only to remain vacant for twelve years until the entire complex was sold to Pritam Singh, a developer. In turn, Singh turned the Little White House over to the state of Florida in exchange for property easements and other rights. It was after that transaction that the initial restoration of the house began, the largest measure of it privately funded by Singh, with curatorial work by the Miami historian Arva Moore Parks. In recent years a new curatorial process was started and it remains ongoing, including contributions from both preservationists and Truman scholars, both adding to the wealth of knowledge of this important American landmark.

Charles Deering Estate
1899 and 1922, Miami

On this estate, architecture was not the end result, but was instead the starting place from which one could inhabit a rich landscape. Charles Deering's interests centered on the botanical splendor of the 308 acres he owned, the art that he collected over his lifetime, and the visits of family and friends who shared his pleasures.

In 1913, Deering (1852–1927), the retired chairman of the board of the International Harvester Company, began to assemble former land-grant property in a town then called Cutler, some fifteen miles south of Miami. At the time, Deering already owned 212 acres in Miami's Buena Vista section, a property he turned into a botanical paradise, but he determined that the Cutler property was a vastly more important natural resource. A single structure, a lively hotel called the Richmond Cottage after its owners S. H. Richmond and

his wife, Edith, stood on the site. Deering bought the Richmond Cottage in 1916, remodeled the hotel as a residence, and in 1922 commissioned the stone building that became the main house.

His architect, Phineas Paist (1875–1937) had come from Philadelphia to work on Vizcaya, the estate of Charles's younger stepbrother, James Deering, after the original architect, F. Burrall Hoffman, left for military service in France. At Cutler, Paist introduced classical principles, using local materials to weave together architectural tradition, and the unique materials and imagery of the Cutler experience. For example, a long view of the entrance suggests a traditional column order, but on closer inspection, the carved native limestone capitals are revealed to be entirely unique, each representing one of the exotic or native creatures that Deering had collected for his estate at Buena Vista (Deering sold this latter estate

in 1925 for what the *New York Times* called the largest single real estate transaction in the south).

Paist drew upon the drama of the expansive vistas across Biscayne Bay, although Deering found his greatest pleasure in the trees. When Paist wrote to Deering to suggest trimming the foliage to open second-floor views of the north shoreline, the reply came back quickly that the trees were to be preserved.

Cutler remained a private property until 1985, when—with the assistance of the state of Florida—Miami-Dade County acquired what is now a 444-acre estate and began the process of assessment with a full-scale restoration effort after the destruction resulting from Hurricane Andrew in 1992. Today, the Deering Estate is the site of a broad range of activities that share the living history of the site, as well as the story of the house and its owner. The county's stewardship carries Deering's commitment to this unique landscape into the future. The estate is a testament to the determination of its original owner and his team of dedicated botanists, designers, and builders, as well as a later generation of preservationists and conservationists.

43

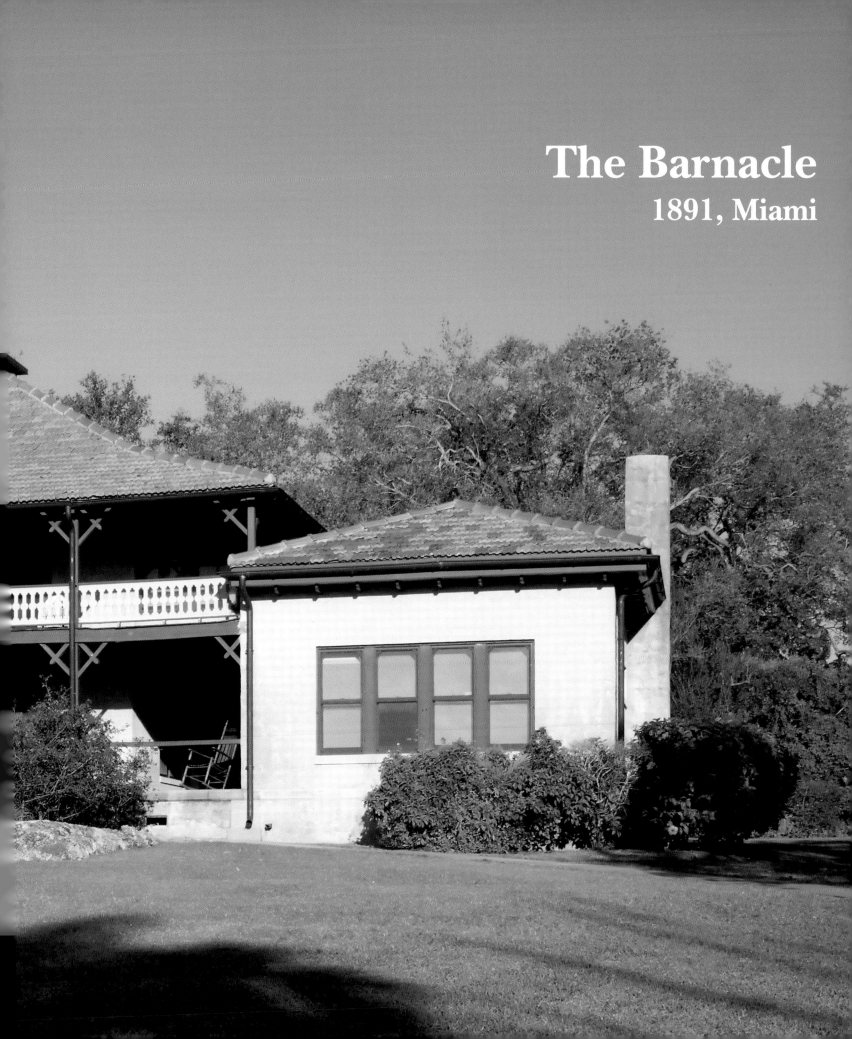

The Barnacle
1891, Miami

PREVIOUS PAGES
In the summer of 1891, C. J. Peacock, Joe Frow, and Ben Newbold built the Barnacle facing it toward the prevailing southeastern breezes of Biscayne Bay.

ABOVE
In 1908 the bungalow was raised up an entire floor and the staircase was added to connect the levels of the new two-story structure.

RIGHT
The first-floor living room features a fireplace framed with saw-cut oolitic limestone with hand-hewn edges.

I n 1877 Biscayne Bay was a true wilderness and Ralph Middleton Munroe believed that "no more isolated region was to be found in the country, and scarcely any less productive." The Seminoles lived at the edge of the Everglades, then very close to the western boundary of Coconut Grove. The only industry of note was the unsustainable production of an arrowrootlike substance from the roots of the *zamia,* an ancient plant found in the scrub of the native pinelands. The curiosities and newness of the landscape and its people enchanted Munroe.

Born in New York City and raised on Staten Island, Munroe (1851–1933) seems an unlikely candidate for pioneer life on Miami's Biscayne Bay. His grandfather, William Munroe, manufactured the first lead pencil in the United States. The young Munroe grew up with the Vanderbilt children in New York, learned to play croquet in Concord with Ralph Waldo Emerson's daughter, Ellen, and went to boarding school with Louis C. Tiffany, among others. After classes in mechanical drawing at Columbia and stints at the New York Rubber Co. and the Russell File Co., Munroe realized that his true calling was the sea.

When his young wife was diagnosed with tuberculosis, Munroe set out with her for Biscayne Bay. The trip ended tragically with her death, along with the death of the infant daughter they had left behind. Five years later, Munroe finally decided to leave New York permanently and returned to Coconut Grove. He built a boathouse

PREVIOUS PAGES
The octagonal central room of the original bungalow served as the dining room. Ralph Munroe described the space as "always airy and comfortable." Ventilation was aided by opening the cupola to release hot air and draw the cooler bay breezes through the house.

NEAR RIGHT
Jessie Wirth Munroe's Singer sewing machine occupies a sunny second-story niche.

FAR RIGHT
The morning sun provides an ideal alarm clock for the Munroe's bedroom, which opens to an expansive southeasterly view across Biscayne Bay.

first, and then, in the summer of 1891, construction commenced on the house known as the Barnacle.

The frame for the Barnacle was constructed of timber retrieved from shipwrecks and milled on the site. The foundation was built of the tough and impermeable local pine made stronger with a coating of pitch. The entire frame was bolted together to resist hurricane-force winds. Finishes—the siding, flooring, ceiling, shingles, and millwork—were imported from Pensacola.

In 1900, Munroe married Jessie Wirth and within three years the family had grown to include a daughter, Patty, and a son, Wirth. As the family grew, the house grew too, most dramatically with an entirely new first floor, and later a library for Munroe. From its position high on the limestone ridge, the Barnacle survived the 1926 hurricane without significant damage and two years later was remodeled once more, this time clad in a stucco finish. What was lost in 1926 was the boathouse with all of Munroe's drawings and files, models, and tools. The family remained secure in the Barnacle after Munroe's death (1933) and Jessie's death in 1940. The Munroe family sold the house to the state of Florida in 1973. Today the Barnacle remains the last bit of evidence of the earliest Coconut Grove waterfront. Amidst the bustle of Coconut Grove's increased urbanization, the Barnacle makes it possible for a visitor to sit on the porch, shaded from the heat and light of the day, and feel the breeze that so enchanted Munroe, inviting the imagination to consider his alternative—life in the untamed tropics.

Merrick House
1910, Coral Gables

PREVIOUS PAGES
*Coral Gables house,
the Merrick family
homestead, was built
from local oolitic
limestone, commonly
called "coral rock."*

ABOVE
*An ornate wooden
archway frames the view
into the living room.*

OPPOSITE
*The entry hall features
artwork by both Althea
Fink Merrick and her
brother, artist Denman
Fink. Near the doorway
is a hat rack that Althea
brought from Duxbury,
Massachusetts, when
the Merrick family
moved to Florida.*

T his serene rock house is among the earli-
est intact buildings in South Florida. It was designed by
Althea Fink Merrick, who lived there with her husband,
the Reverend Solomon Merrick, and her family, among
them their son George, the founder and creator of the
city of Coral Gables. George Merrick lived in this coral
house from 1910, when he was twenty-four, until he was
married six years later; he and his wife Eunice moved
back again briefly in 1930. The Merrick family moved to
the area in 1899 to 160 acres known as the Gregory
Homestead. They settled there with their family of eight
in a small wooden cottage on the rocky land, which they
bought for $1,100. Subsequently, they planted grapefruit
groves.

The Merricks began turning the little cottage into a
house of larger dimensions. The dates of construction are
somewhat uncertain, but historian Arva Moore Parks has
concluded that the foundations were set in 1907, though
the house itself was not completed until 1910. The house
is constructed of the native oolitic limestone that was in
abundance early in the last century, and has broad roof
overhangs and graceful porches. The Merricks called it
Coral Gables (alluding to the oolitic limestone known as
"coral rock" it was made of and the gables it featured).
This, of course, was the name their eldest son, George,
would adopt when, starting just a decade later, he
planned his dream city. His ambitious plan was to create
a near-utopian "City Beautiful" in Coral Gables, "not a
thing of the moment, of the year, or even of the passing
period, but a wonderful monument."

However, a devastating hurricane in the fall of 1926,
coupled with a rail embargo (which prevented building
materials from being shipped to South Florida), and an
unsupportable building boom across the entire state created what was termed "the bust." Florida, especially

PREVIOUS PAGES
Archways frame the view into the dining room from the living room. Objects in the room include a portrait plate and china painted by Althea Merrick, as well as a painting by her son Richard.

ABOVE
Though this room is now interpreted as George's office, it had been the bedroom of two of his brothers, Richard and Charles. The desk belonged to their father, Solomon Merrick, and was originally in the living room.

RIGHT
The living room at the Coral Gables House features a baby grand piano and comfortable furniture. Beyond the living room is a sun porch that was enclosed in the 1920s.

South Florida, plunged early into the Depression that by 1929 would wrack the entire country. During this time, Merrick lost control of the Coral Gables enterprise, and as the Depression deepened, the once-prosperous Merrick family fell on hard times. George's sister Ethel turned their home into a boarding house called Merrick Manor, which it was until 1961. The city of Coral Gables took it over in 1976.

The house today is known as Coral Gables House. In recent years the house has overcome serious problems, including mold and buckling floors. A team of architects and historians sought out photos and all other available documentation to bring the house back to life; floor joists and oolitic limestone pilings were replaced and 120 linear feet of new foundation was poured. The heating, cooling, and electrical systems were upgraded. Ultimately, all the wood on the first floor had to be replaced with the closest possible match to the original, reclaimed Central Florida river pine. After analysis, the decision was made to leave the woodwork throughout the house bare, as photos showed it to have been early in the last century. Paint studies showed that the walls had a finish akin to Venetian plaster, so they were stripped down and redone.

Vizcaya
1916, Miami

V izcaya is a treasure trove of architecture, landscape, and art. Visitors today are astonished by the richness and pedigree of the villa, grounds, and interiors. Operated as a museum by Miami-Dade County, this National Historic Landmark offers a glimpse of the life of James Deering (1859–1925), world-renowned industrialist and innovator in farm machinery. In the 1930s after his death, Deering's nieces, Marion Deering McCormick (1886–1965) and Barbara Deering Danielson (1888–1987), found that Miami's active hurricane seasons of the 1930s and 40s made the operation of the estate, which had been opened to the public, difficult to continue. Subsequently, much of the property was sold to the Diocese of St. Augustine, in anticipation of the soon-to-beformed Miami Diocese, which later built a high school and church, selling the remaining land to a hospital and housing development that surround Vizcaya today. By 1952, the county reached an agreement with the Deering heirs to acquire the villa and later the farm village, and in 1955 the family donated the original furnishings and art to the county to open Vizcaya as a museum.

One of Florida's most magical places, Vizcaya represents the work of a motivated and sophisticated owner, and his capable team of designers and builders. James Deering spent his business life in the Deering Manufacturing Company, founded by his father William, followed by the directorship of a larger company that was formed when Deering Manufacturing merged with Cyrus McCormick, its leading competitor. Later James served as vice president of International Harvester, the company that resulted from the merger financed by J. P. Morgan; James Deering continued as a lifelong member of the board. By 1909, however, he began a new avocation as a

PRECEDING PAGES
A view of the villa Vizcaya from Biscayne Bay.

OPPOSITE
The east loggia, along the principle views, is framed with four sets of quadruple columns. A seventeenth-century Venetian floor inspired the marble medallion and pattern. The caravel, a symbol James Deering chose for Vizcaya, is suspended from the ceiling.

ABOVE
The wood paneling (boiserie) of the music room is laden with gilt and lacquer, while the ceiling and painted canvas panels come from a Milanese palace, setting the scene for the seventeenth-century Italian spinet and Adam harp.

collector and patron of the arts. At the same time, his visits to the family's Coconut Grove home inspired his affection for the climate, topography, and landscape. An early member of the Biscayne Bay Yacht Club, Deering had an intimate knowledge of the coastline and an appreciation for the intertwining of water and land that distinguishes the South Florida coast and ultimately he chose a site on the Coconut Grove waterfront for his winter home.

Well traveled, with a house in Chicago and an apartment in Paris, Deering began planning the design of his winter residence with the assistance of Paul Chalfin (1874–1959), who is generally considered to be the design impresario of Vizcaya. Deering initially hired Chalfin, a Harvard graduate, recipient of the Prix de Rome, a painter, and former curator of the Boston Museum of Fine Arts, to assist on a European excursion. Acting as an interior designer and acquisitions adviser, Chalfin's responsibilities expanded. He engaged the full design team, beginning with F. Burall Hoffman Jr. (1882–1980), who had studied at Harvard University and L'Ecole des Beaux-Arts, and had begun his career with the New York firm Carrère & Hastings as the primary architect. For the gardens, Chalfin hired Diego Suarez (1888–1974), who had studied engineering in Bogotá until his father's death, when he returned with his mother to her native Italy and studied architecture. Suarez had originally met Chalfin and Deering at La Pietra, the Florentine villa and garden of Suarez's friend and mentor Arthur Acton, well known for his restoration of the classical garden in Italy. With Chalfin in charge and in constant consultation with Deering, the team of principal designers commenced work in 1912, and construction began in 1914. Deering opened the house to his family and friends in late December of 1916. An immediate sensation, the villa was featured in *Architectural Review*, *Harper's Bazaar*, *Town & Country*, and *Vogue* in 1917. The tropics suffused the house, especially in the garden within the central courtyard which opened to the sky, where William Patterson of *Town & Country* described the sounds "heard, remote and nearby, of dropping water, of falling water, of brokenly rushing water in fountains; and glimpses of a gallery beneath broad overhanging roofs give a hint of the importance of the courtyard in plan."

ABOVE
*Next to the sitting room
and overlooking
Biscayne Bay, James
Deering's bedroom
continued the French
empire theme with
mahogany furnishings
with gold-leafed bronze
fittings. The canopied
bed is said to have come
from the Château
de Malmaison.*

ABOVE RIGHT
*The tented ceiling of
the master bathroom
is made of embroidered
linen, supported by a
Greek key-patterned frieze.*

OPPOSITE
*The "Cathay" guest
room, named for a poetic
term for China,
represents a Venetian
vision of chinoiserie.*

Deering positioned the villa directly on the bay front, an unusual choice for the region since most houses were placed on the highest ground atop the limestone ridge, and given an expansive distance between the house and the bay. The result of this choice was a majestic facade toward the sea, inspired by the Villa Rezzonico and embellished with a waterfront barge. Originally framed with a lattice summerhouse and garden at one end and a teahouse to the south, the barge was called "the proudest architectural creation of my life," by Suarez who wrote that it was "inspired by the famous barge at the Villa Borromeo at Isola Bella on Lago Maggiore in Northern Italy." Stirling Calder designed the sculptural elements of the barge, completing the figures on site. Period photographs show that the barge was, as Suarez conceived it, an island garden.

The interior rooms of Vizcaya are lush with the fruits of Deering's travels with Chalfin. Architectural elements, such as doors and surrounds, window frames, chimney-pieces and mantles, brackets and beams were imported from the grand palaces of Europe. Rooms were planned around the major pieces and mocked-up in a warehouse before installation in the villa. What is particularly

RIGHT
Venetian gondola poles mark this view of the lattice teahouse, positioned at the end of the Venetian bridge.

BELOW
Originally conceived as an island garden, the "barge" features a series of figures sculpted by A. Stirling Calder with later assistance from Gaston Lachaise.

OPPOSITE
The woods form the backdrop for two of the four gazebos that mark the edges of the parterre. Renowned Philadelphia iron artist Samuel Yellin provided the balustrade between the stucco piers.

interesting about Vizcaya is that the effect of this museum-quality planning of interior furnishing is not, in fact, a museum, but a house.

In Vizcaya today, the sense of domesticity is evident. The appointments are lavish, the materials regal, and yet the overall effect is still personal. Perhaps the juxtaposition of priceless artifacts with local stones, or refined silks, tapestry, and gilt with hand-crafted tile and stucco brings the worldliest elements into a local domain. It is also possible that Chalfin's orchestration of the interiors is simply masterfully done and he consistently made the presence of the owner his foremost goal. However the result was accomplished, the final effect of the suite of grand and cabinetlike rooms, courts, and open loggias is a sense of the life lived in the house, friends and family gathered, artists painting and meeting at the dinner hour, explorations of the lagoons. This interpretation doesn't really require the documentation of a historian; the house itself tells the tale.

El Jardin
1918, Miami

PREVIOUS PAGES
*Positioned atop the
Atlantic limestone ridge,
El Jardin originally
fronted a lawn laced
with Dade County pines
and was centered on a
formal parterre framed
with Italian cypress trees.*

RIGHT
*The design of the living
room is based on sixteenth-
century Spanish
architecture, most
evident in the fireplace
done in the exuberant
Churrigueresque
manner.*

FOLLOWING PAGES
*The courtyard, a forty-
five-foot-square space
with twelfth-century
Sicilian columns topped
with hand-wrought
lanterns, features a
Venetian marble
fountain. A portion of
upper loggia was
enclosed for classroom
space in the 1960s.*

Built along the peak of an ancient ridge
of oolitic limestone, El Jardin was the home of John Bindley, then president of Pittsburgh Steel. El Jardin's architect, Richard Kiehnel (1870–1944) married modern
convenience with the art and architecture of England,
Italy, Spain, and Tunisia to bring the culture of a sophisticated collector to the reality of tropical Florida. The
house, constructed between 1916 and 1918, was outfitted
with ornamental steel doors, windows, and scrollwork;
girded with structural steel; and supplied with electricity
throughout the buildings, gardens, and grounds on its
ten-acre site.

Kiehnel worked with contractor John B. Orr and
craftsmen who had just completed Vizcaya, to build what
Kiehnel described, in a September 1928 article for *Tropical Home and Garden*, as a "progenitor of the modern
Mediterranean style home." The German-born architect
drew upon his extensive travel and studies to create an
"Old World" feel amidst the native pines and palms. The
gatehouse, diminutive and rusticated, introduced many
of the ornamental motifs of the villa, including moldings,
cast columns, and an ornamental soffit. Originally lined
with cast-concrete lanterns, the entrance drive wound
through the gardens, culminating at the terrace facing
the front doors of the villa. Modeled on the doors of the
Palace of Santa Cruz of Toledo, Spain, the great doors

OPPOSITE AND BELOW
The dining room is modeled on the work of the prolific British architect Robert Adam, known for his accomplished ornament. The decorative motifs of urns, leaves, and classical figures were popularly known as the

Etruscan style; however, two centuries of Josiah Wedgwood's similarly figured pottery and porcelain eclipsed Adam's inspiration, thus earning the dining room the nickname of the "Wedgwood room."

FOLLOWING PAGES
Carved sea creatures ornament the arches supported by spiral columns, creating a rusticated limestone base for the terrace.

frame a view through the courtyard that extends out to Biscayne Bay beyond.

The courtyard remains open to the elements, covered only by its original bronze-and-copper screen. In 1961, Carrollton School of the Sacred Heart became the third owner of El Jardin, acquiring the property and all its furnishings. Although the transition to satisfy the needs of a school for students from preschool through twelfth grade demanded adjustments, the school worked to preserve and, as needed, restore the original beauty of El Jardin. With assistance from The Villagers, a group dedicated to the preservation and restoration of historic sites, and later the state of Florida's Bureau of Historic Preservation, the school has fully restored the courtyard, dining room, living room, library, and loggia. Consistent with the country-house era, each room presents a different theme and ornamental motif, ranging from the restrained classicism of Robert Adam to the sumptuous tile of the Moorish loggia.

El Jardin is rich in individually significant detail and ornament. The Bindley crest appears throughout, interwoven with relevant classical elements. A frieze (found on the exterior of the villa, the stair hall, and the second-floor loggia) introduces the griffin, a mythological creature with the lower body of a lion and the upper body of an eagle, believed by the Greeks to guard the gold of Scythia. A symbol of steadfastness, the griffin was a popular figure in the work of Adam; it also appears in the ceiling of the dining room as well as in furniture details. The sunflower, also seen throughout the villa, was known in the seventeenth century as an emblem of gratitude, constancy, and remembrance, while other symbols have specific Christian associations, like the scallop shell, which was associated from the twelfth century forward with the emblems of the pilgrims commemorating the apparition of St. James of Santiago de Compostela. The richness of El Jardin's iconography reinforces its current role in the education of enlightened young women.

79

The Kampong
1928, Miami

David Fairchild, the famed plant explorer who had helped initiate the United States Department of Agriculture's first Office of Foreign Seed and Plant Introduction in Washington, D.C., and Marian, intrepid coexplorer, daughter of Alexander Graham Bell, and granddaughter of telephone investor Gardiner Greene Hubbard of the National Geographic Society, first saw the site of the Kampong in 1916. Fairchild, who had introduced tropical plants to the United States, including "Chinese elms, velvet beans, persimmons, pistachios, Central American avocados, and a host of other important crop plants," was eager for the opportunity to test his discoveries on his own homestead.

A previous owner, Dr. Galt Simmons, who was a country doctor who ministered to the settlers as well as the natives, had—with her husband—built a Dade County pine-frame house with an oolitic limestone fireplace. Eventually this house would be moved elsewhere on the property to accommodate a new, concrete and limestone house for the Fairchild family—Marian, David, their children, and a future generation of grandchildren. But well before the family arrived, in his earliest moments at the Kampong, Fairchild recalled in his memoir, *The World Grows Round My Door*, that he "sat for a long time that morning gazing out to sea, and at the beach of coral and limestone and the low land back of it, which was beginning to be covered with all sorts of wild vegetation."

PREVIOUS PAGES
View of the main Kampong house from the garden.

LEFT
This view of the living room looks towards the fireplace and an antique eighth-century South Asian sculpture mounted above it. The room was furnished by the Kampong's last owner, Catherine (Kay) Sweeney.

85

OPPOSITE
*Garuda, the mythical
birdlike creature of
Hindu and Buddhist
mythology, has long been
a subject of southeast
Asian artists influenced
by Indian traders. Two
garudas were installed
in the lobby and
stairway in the 1990s.
The enormous wood
sculpture above (from
the trunk and roots of a
single litchi tree) was
procured in Bali and
refinished by Miami
wood sculptor Barry
Massin. The solid
rosewood stairwell was
constructed by artisans
in Hong Kong.*

With the guidance of Marian Fairchild, and the expertise of architect Clarence Dean, the compound began to take shape. In 1928 they built the main house with its distinctive arched gateway framing the vista to the bay. Fairchild explained that the name of the property evolved so that "by the time we finished putting up houses and moving shacks about, there were so many buildings on the place that it suggested a little village—a Javanese *kampong*, and 'The Kampong' it became."

Blending local building materials with details drawn from their travels, the Fairchilds created a stage set for the active life they conducted in the garden. After David Fairchild's death, Marian continued to live at the Kampong, initially with her daughter and son-in-law, Barbara and Leonard Muller, and eventually with her grand-daughter, Helene Muller Pancoast, and her husband, Lester. When Marian Fairchild died in 1962, the Kampong found an ideal owner in Catherine (Kay) and Edward Sweeney, who acquired the property in 1963. For the next twenty years, Kay Sweeney maintained the Kampong to honor its history and preserve its role in tropical horticulture. In 1984, she donated the property to what is now the National Tropical Botanical Garden, an institution with four gardens and three preserves in Hawaii. The National Tropical Botanical Garden, through its efforts in Hawaii and at the Kampong, is dedicated to the conservation of tropical plant diversity, with a focus on rare and endangered species, a goal most evident in the Fairchilds's Florida home.

ABOVE
*The soft stone sculpture
of traditional Balinese
mythical figures that
ornament the door-
surround was crafted in
Bali from Catherine
Sweeney's instructions
and installed in 1969.*

FOLLOWING PAGES
*The entrance gateway of
the Kampong opens to a
terrace garden with views
toward Biscayne Bay.*

Stranahan House
1901, Fort Lauderdale

T he Fort Lauderdale that Frank and Ivy Stranahan knew a century ago was virgin turf, a place of raw, exotic beauty. Only a handful of settlers lived there (fifty-two in the 1900 census count), and the settlement was largely clustered along the New River; the residents of Southern Florida in those years faced difficult odds in a hot, buggy, isolated place. Yet, amid these circumstances, the Stranahans created a place of extraordinary grace and elegance, a two-story house with wide verandas wrapping around it. Over the years it served as a post office, trading post, community center, town hall, and restaurant, as well as a residence for the Stranahans.

Built of indigenous Dade County pine in 1901, it is the oldest structure in Broward County. The house was expanded over the years; as it stands now, the house represents the period of 1913 to 1915, by which time the Stranahans had installed electrical wiring, indoor plumbing, and running water as amenities. The house has bay windows and wide porches, and is painted to match the original color scheme of white with green trim.

Frank Stranahan arrived in Fort Lauderdale in 1896, and it was at the site of the Stranahan House that he built the dock for the barge-ferry that crossed the New River for the just-built "Dixie Highway" that was to run from Lantana, in Palm Beach County, to North Miami, in what is now Miami-Dade County. Stranahan, who was also Fort

PREVIOUS PAGES
A timeless view of the Stranahan House shows it from Fort Lauderdale's New River, the way in which traders originally reached it in the years just after the turn of the twentieth century.

LEFT
The parlor has the original fireplace. Local shipbuilder Ed King constructed the house using sturdy Dade County pine for the walls.

ABOVE
A view into the dining room.

None of the Stranahan House's furniture is original to it, but the current furnishings were selected to reflect what it would have looked like in the early years of the twentieth century.

ABOVE
The stairwell to the second floor was constructed to offer views back to the rooms below.

ABOVE RIGHT
A writing desk sits in a corner of the dining room.

OPPOSITE
A view into the parlor from the dining room.

Lauderdale's first postmaster and president of the town's first bank, built the house as a trading post for both the Fort Lauderdale pioneer and Seminole communities.

His wife (they were married in 1900) was Fort Lauderdale's first schoolteacher, Ivy Julia Cromartie. Together they transformed Stranahan House from a lonely outpost to a lively community center hosting dances, socials, and other events. After operating it as a commercial and social center, the Stranahans finally moved into the house in 1906. For the next two decades, the Stranahans prospered, but in 1929 Frank committed suicide after his bank failed. Ivy Stranahan remained in the house until her death in 1971, leasing out the ground floor as a restaurant.

Two years after her death, the house was listed on the National Register of Historic Places. In 1979, the Fort Lauderdale Historical Society assumed ownership of the house, and subsequently a separate nonprofit was formed to operate it. The house was restored incorporating appropriate period furniture, as most of the original interiors had been lost. It now operates as a house museum that bears testimony to early twentieth-century life in Fort Lauderdale.

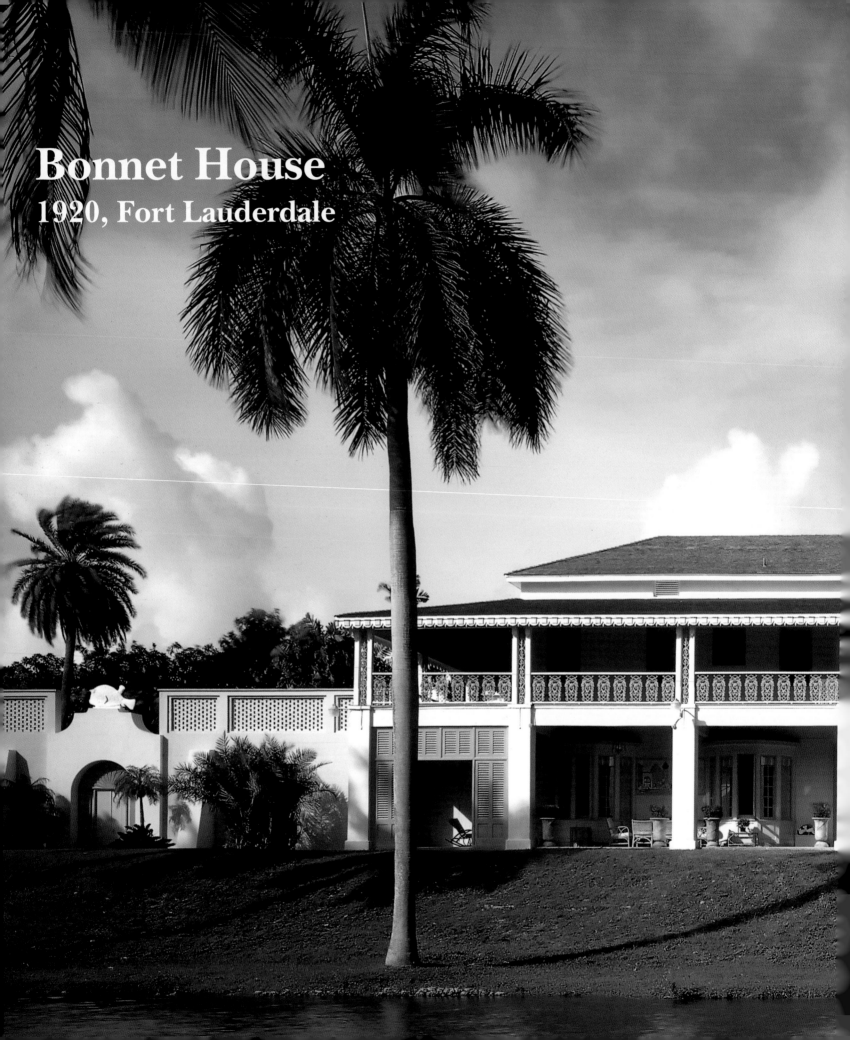

Bonnet House
1920, Fort Lauderdale

T he history of Fort Lauderdale's beach is long lost. The charming Las Olas Inn, the precursor to Bonnet House, was demolished in 1958, and the neighboring beach club, designed by the young Francis Abreu, was razed in the 1960s, yielding to what is now the International Swimming Hall of Fame. With pavement reaching to the very edge of the beach, it is hard to imagine that the coast was ever a cool and verdant landscape offering shade and refuge. Yet that is exactly what Chicago lawyer Hugh Taylor Birch discovered in the mid-1890s, and why he purchased three miles of oceanfront property, the present-day Hugh Taylor Birch State Park, and to the south, Bonnet House.

Although he led an active social life at his Michigan Avenue home in Chicago, in 1898 Birch built a two-room frame cottage on his Florida beachfront. By 1913, Birch's wife, Maria Root, had died, leaving him with their only surviving child, Helen. A published composer and poet, Helen frequently joined her father at the Villa Moonflower, very near the hunting lodge that became the Las Olas Inn. Correspondence with the famed plant explorer David Fairchild confirms the family's interest in the native and exotic landscape, as well as their affection for the simplicity of an outdoor life surrounded by beautiful weather, the sea, and an extraordinary array of plants and wildlife.

PREVIOUS PAGES
Bonnet House presides over a sloping lawn that leads to the freshwater Bonnet Slough.

LEFT
The drawing room's gilded spiral pilasters and painted rocaille or Muschelwork above the door and windows express Frederic Bartlett's eclectic compositions of refined and rustic elements, three-dimensional ornament, and trompe l'oeil.

ABOVE
Originally planned for Helen Birch Bartlett, the music room features an 1871 Steinway square piano, the Veiled Lady *by Milanese sculptor Giuseppe Croff (1810–1869), and a faux-marble floor painted by Frederic Bartlett.*

In January of 1919 Helen married painter and muralist Frederic Clay Bartlett. As a wedding gift, Birch, gave the couple a thirty-five-acre parcel of his oceanfront property. Very soon after, and with the assistance of Birch, who remained on site to supervise construction, the couple began to build Bonnet House, named for the lily of nearby Bonnet Slough.

Bartlett was, in his time, a well-known artist, responsible for the interior of Chicago's University Club, including the stained-glass windows and ceiling panels of the Michigan Room. In 1895, along with the architect Howard Van Doren Shaw, Bartlett built the "House in the Woods" in Geneva, Wisconsin, for his father Adolphus Clay Bartlett, who had been a charter director of the Northern Trust Company in Chicago. Organized around a courtyard, "House in the Woods" suggests the future plan for Bonnet House, though Florida's benevolent winter climate made it possible for Bartlett to open a series of loggias around the central courtyard and to create open porches overlooking the principal views.

The architecture of Bonnet House looks to Mediterranean references, although not directly, as much as it's derived from the German interpretation of classicism, which Bartlett studied during his travels and residence abroad. Inspired by Chicago's Columbian Exposition in 1893, Bartlett began his studies at the Royal Academy in Munich, and later moved to Paris to study, and subsequently work, in the studio of James McNeill Whistler. Bartlett brought his vast visual repertoire to life in the composition and design of Bonnet House as the home of his near contemporary, the Swedish painter Carl Larsson, has been described.

Bounded by the New River Sound and the Florida East Coast Canal on the west, and Bonnet Slough and the Atlantic Ocean to the east, the property hosted the entire coastal ecosystem, from mangrove to coastal hardwood to hammock. The Bartletts arranged the house with respect toward this untouched wilderness, sympathetic to the interests of Birch, who lived with them at the house and offered counsel. In 1925 Helen Birch Bartlett died, and for the next six years Birch wintered on the property while Bartlett traveled. In 1931, Frederic Bartlett married Evelyn Fortune Lilly, former wife of the son of wealthy pharmaceutical businessman Eli Lilly Jr., in Beverly, Massachusetts. She worked with Bartlett to develop her hand as a painter and watercolorist, and together they began to enhance the interiors of Bonnet House, including the creation of several fanciful pavilions, the *wunderkammer* shell collection, and later, a tentlike structure overlooking the pond, and a theater at the opposite end of the lagoon. They also sketched and built a stone fountain for the south *allée*.

The Bartletts extended their art into the elements of the garden as well. Designing landscapes as distinctive

outdoor rooms, they brought painterly concepts of contrast and variety to a shady *allée* that opened to a sunny clearing, heightening the contrast between the spaces further through the dark-trunk trees of the woods, and the bright, reflective, arid plant collection of the clearing. Designed elements worked together with landscape for scenic effect, as the aviary reinforced the tropical motif of the courtyard, while the more restrained décor of the veranda responded to the broad lawn along the edge of the eastern waterway.

Revised through artistic interpretation and accommodation to local influence, Bonnet House presents a uniquely tropical language, where the lively expression of baroque ornament finds form with whimsical impressions of sea creatures and exotic plants. Within the rooms of Bonnet House, the Florida that enchanted the Birches and Bartletts is fully revived. Although the estate and neighboring park are the last survivors of their era, the power of place prevails over the present day to reveal the wonder that once was.

OPPOSITE
The veranda shades the drawing room and overlooks Bonnet Slough. The second floor offers views to the Atlantic Ocean.

ABOVE
Although the tiered fountain replaced the original shell and rock sculpture by Frederic Bartlett, the keystone edges of the pool and court remain.

Cà d'Zan
1926, Sarasota

C à d'Zan, John and Mable Ringling's ode to Venice on Sarasota Bay, was at one point one of the most famous houses in America, widely photographed and published. Then it was almost lost. By the late 1980s, this once-sumptuous mansion was a shambles, the result of benign neglect and even a certain amount of abuse. The house is now fastidiously restored and lovingly curated, the result of a prodigious effort by the staff of the Ringling Museum and the architects and craftsmen who worked on it.

John and Mable Ringling had first seen Sarasota in 1909, and, in 1911, bought their first house there on twenty acres fronting Sarasota Bay. Despite the populist source of the Ringling fortune, the couple was well trav-

eled, and had schooled themselves in the arts. One of seven brothers, John Ringling acquired his fortune from the circus empire his family developed, enhanced by the acquisition of the Barnum & Bailey Circus. He and Mable made frequent trips to Europe to find new circus acts and buy art; the Ringlings became major art collectors in the course of their travels.

By 1924, the Ringlings had added to their Sarasota land holdings and were ready to commission a house of their own there. To design it they ultimately selected Dwight James Baum, whose practice was in Riverdale, New York. Baum (1886–1939) had gained a reputation for his country houses, but was also active in the Florida boom. Mable Ringling asked for a Venetian palazzo, and

PREVIOUS PAGES
The enclosed court with its terra-cotta mezzanine columns and balustrade was the main area for entertaining; it had a Steinway concert grand piano and an Aeolian Duo-Art organ. The court was filled with numerous pieces of furniture and objects from the John Jacob Astor and William K. Vanderbilt estates.

OPPOSITE
An overhead view of the thirty-one-foot Pecky cypress ceiling painted in gouache by Robert Webb, Jr., with scenes imitating an old Venetian palazzo. A crystal chandelier purchased from the old Waldorf=Astoria in 1929 dominates the space.

ABOVE
Working in his New York studio, the painter Willy Pogany created the colorful scene Carnival in Venice, *a ceiling mural on shaped canvas.*

Portraits of John and Mable Ringling are the central feature, and there is also a self-portrait of Pogany dancing with a paintbrush.

Baum complied, if at times (according to Aaron de Groft and David C. Weeks in their study of the mansion) grudgingly. The end result was a work that in its form followed the pattern of the more typical American country houses of the time, but had Venetian Gothic elements that could be traced to such hotels as the Danieli and the Bauer Grunwald, as well as details taken from the Doge's Palace and the Cà d'Oro. The house was completed in 1926.

The thirty-two-room house sits on the vast grounds that include the Florentine- and Roman-inspired Ringling Museum, as well as newer additions to the complex. It has glazed terra-cotta-tile cladding; the tile, selected by Mable Ringling, is used in some profusion both inside and out. On the interior, other decorative details abound. The painter Robert Webb Jr., who studied with John Singer Sargent, was responsible for many of the ceilings, including the lavish dining room. In the ballroom, however, the Hungarian-born artist Willy Pogany, who was chiefly known as a set designer for both the Ziegfeld Follies and the Metropolitan Opera, was commissioned to create a work entitled *Dancers of the Nations*. Pogany also decorated the ceiling of the third-floor game room.

Cà d'Zan's focal point—and the only significantly sized room in the entire house—is its grand court. One arrives at the house and enters off an entrance foyer, that leads to the dramatic three-story court, and, in turn, this

The reception room is actually the east side of the ballroom; it has Asian teak flooring and gilded serpentine columns from Venice. The Napoleon III Aubusson carpet dates to the 1870s.

The formal dining room has black-walnut paneling, which was purchased at auction and installed in the house in 1925. The walnut dining table was created by Jules Allard and Sons and the silver-plated lighting is by E. F. Caldwell of New York. The Irish-Georgian mirrors are dated 1755.

The gilded, coffered ceiling frames the paintings that constitute Dancers of Nations *by Willy Pogany. On the walls are neoclassical English mirrors and early Venetian mirrors.*

ABOVE
*Mable Ringling's
bedroom featured
Parisian furniture in
the rococo style and
hand-painted linen
walls.*

RIGHT
*John Ringling's bedroom
furniture was also made
in Paris and is one of
two known versions of a
suite created for
Napoleon III, the other
is now at Malmaison.
The ceiling painting,*
Dawn Driving Away
Darkness, *was painted
by Jacob De Wit in
1735. The neoclassical
architectural elements
are all gold leaf.*

vast space opens back out onto the bay, creating both drama and intimacy.

The house was equipped with an elevator—the first such in a Florida private residence—but the primary ascent to the second floor was a curved Carrara marble grand staircase. The Ringlings purchased furniture, tapestries, doors, and other accoutrements at sales in New York as some of the country's great earlier houses were being dispersed; both furniture and art, including tapestries, came from such sources as the residences of Mrs. William Astor on Fifth Avenue in New York, George Crocker in Mahwah, New Jersey, and George Jay Gould. The rooms were described by Ringling historian Weeks as having "a fashionable surfeit of splendor."

Throughout, however, splendor and sass hold equal billing. Cà d'Zan is simultaneously lavish and quirky, as the Pogany ceiling paintings attest.

Mable Ringling died in 1929 and John in 1936. Upon his death, John willed his collection of art, the house, and grounds to the state of Florida. When it was under state control the Cà d'Zan suffered its steep decline. Renovation work was under way by 2000, when control of the entire complex was transferred to Florida State University, and the careful restoration of the house was made a top priority; it was completed in 2002.

RIGHT

Cà d'Zan's waterside approach was fashioned after the Doge's Palace in Venice. John Ringling's 125-foot yacht the Zalophus was moored off the lower dock.

The 12,000-square-foot marble terrace was created in a chevron pattern and provided an enormous dance floor for the Ringling's extravagant gatherings.

TOP

The belvedere looks out onto the vast acreage that John Ringling once owned. Its decorative features are glazed terra-cotta in motifs of flora and fauna. A frieze surrounds the tower with depictions of the zodiac.

ABOVE

Cà d'Zan rises eighty-one feet above Sarasota Bay and has 36,000 square feet of interior space for its fifty-six rooms.

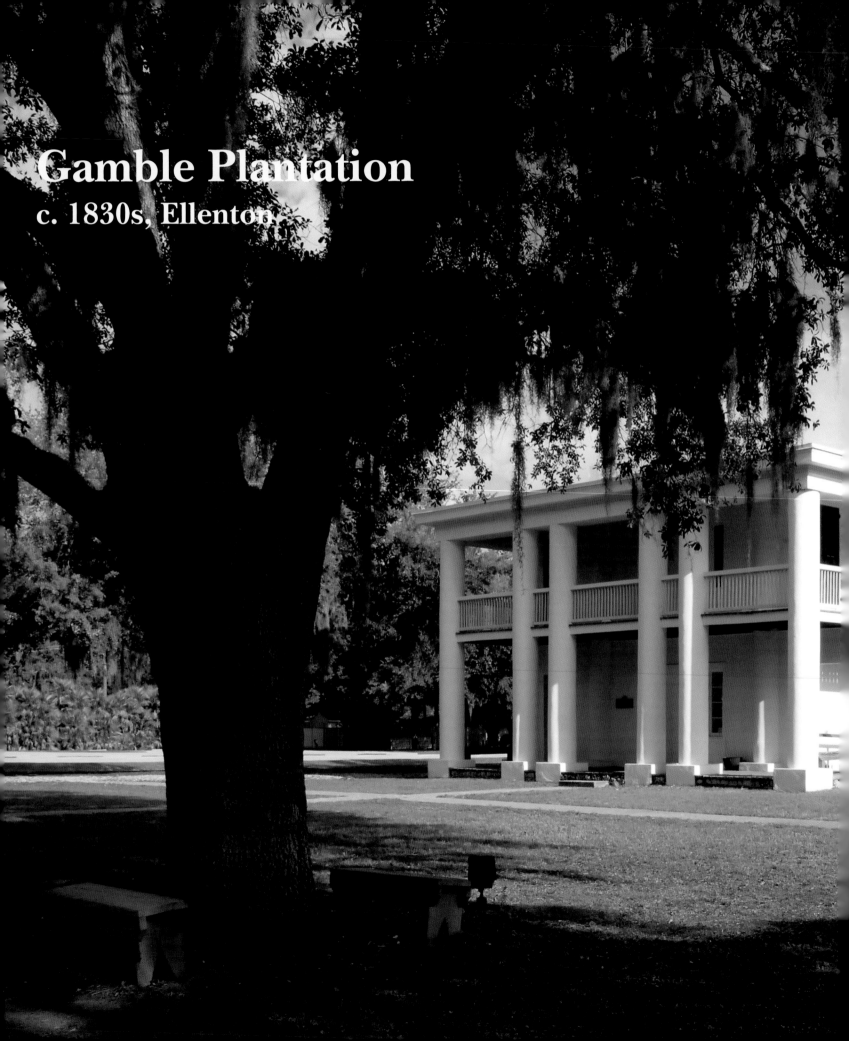

Gamble Plantation
c. 1830s, Ellenton

PREVIOUS PAGES
*This easterly view of the
Gamble plantation house
shows the nineteenth-
century water cistern
that has survived into
the twenty-first century.*

ABOVE
*The east loggia with its
sturdy columns and
protective roof.*

RIGHT
*A portrait of Robert
Gamble hangs over
the mantle in the
dining room.*

The owner of the Gamble Plantation, Major Robert Gamble, settled there after the Second Seminole War. Gamble had determined, in 1844, to establish a sugar plantation along the Manatee River and purchased three thousand five hundred acres northeast of Braden-ton. He was one of a number of such settlers, who opted in that decade to try to bring Northern Florida's planta-tion economy south, but with a reliance on sugar rather than the cotton that drove the state's earliest plantations. Paul Eugen Camp describes the area as a study in con-trasts, the large-scale plantations and complex slave econ-omy juxtaposed against what was comparative wilderness.

In 1888, Gamble wrote a reminiscence for the *Florid-ian* newspaper and described the surroundings this way: "There were no settlements in the interior; the nearest town, then a mere village, was Tampa, some forty miles to the north, and it was only accessible by water, there being no roads. Our only communication with the outer world was a small sloop of about 12 tons, which was built by one of the artisans above alluded to. The boat once in a month to six weeks plied to the port of Saint Marks, bring-ing us our letters and papers, all supplies of provisions and other matters, and carrying the few passengers who passed between these points."

In the memoir he wrote that "most of the rich lands on the Manatee were in the hands of men who about the end of the war availed themselves of an Act of Congress styles [*sic*] the 'Armed Occupation Law.' Under this law every armed man who occupied a quarter section under the provisions of this act for five consecutive years, erecting a house and putting into cultivation during that period five acres of land, would on proof of compliance with the conditions of his permit receive from the Government a deed to his 160 acres. Upon my arrival I found the dense hammock tenanted by intelligent men, nearly all mechanics of great skill. There were blacksmiths, boiler makers, workers in iron in the higher branches of the art, cabinetmakers, carpenters, bricklayers, etc., etc., and by availing myself of the services of these men, I was enabled to overcome, when I commenced the erection of my buildings, what otherwise, in a country so entirely cut off and remote from the resources of civilization could have proved almost insuperable obstacles."

With his slaves numbering some three hundred, Gamble grew sugarcane, molasses, citrus, grapes, and olives, which were shipped to New Orleans. His classic-revival house was built of red brick and tabby, with walls that measured almost two feet in depth, a strategy for keeping cool in the summer and warm in winter. The house was designed with two wings to capture cross breezes and broad double verandas to keep the sun out. The house also had a water catchment system that channeled rain from the gutters; it has survived since 1844. Gamble's tenure at the plantation was comparatively short-lived, however; in 1856 he sold it and returned to what he termed "Central Florida," actually Tallahassee. During the Civil War, the mill itself was destroyed but the house was not. Ultimately, the postwar owners of the house—the Patten family—fell on hard times, and the house was taken over by a fertilizer company that in the early 1920s stored manure there. In 1925 the Daughters of the Confederacy purchased and restored the Gamble house, which, with its grounds, is now part of the Florida State Parks system.

OPPOSITE
A horsehair upholstered rocking chair sits in Robert Gamble's bedroom.

ABOVE
This bedroom with its four-poster bed acknowledges Confederate Secretary of State Judah P. Benjamin who sought refuge on the plantation near the end of the Civil War.

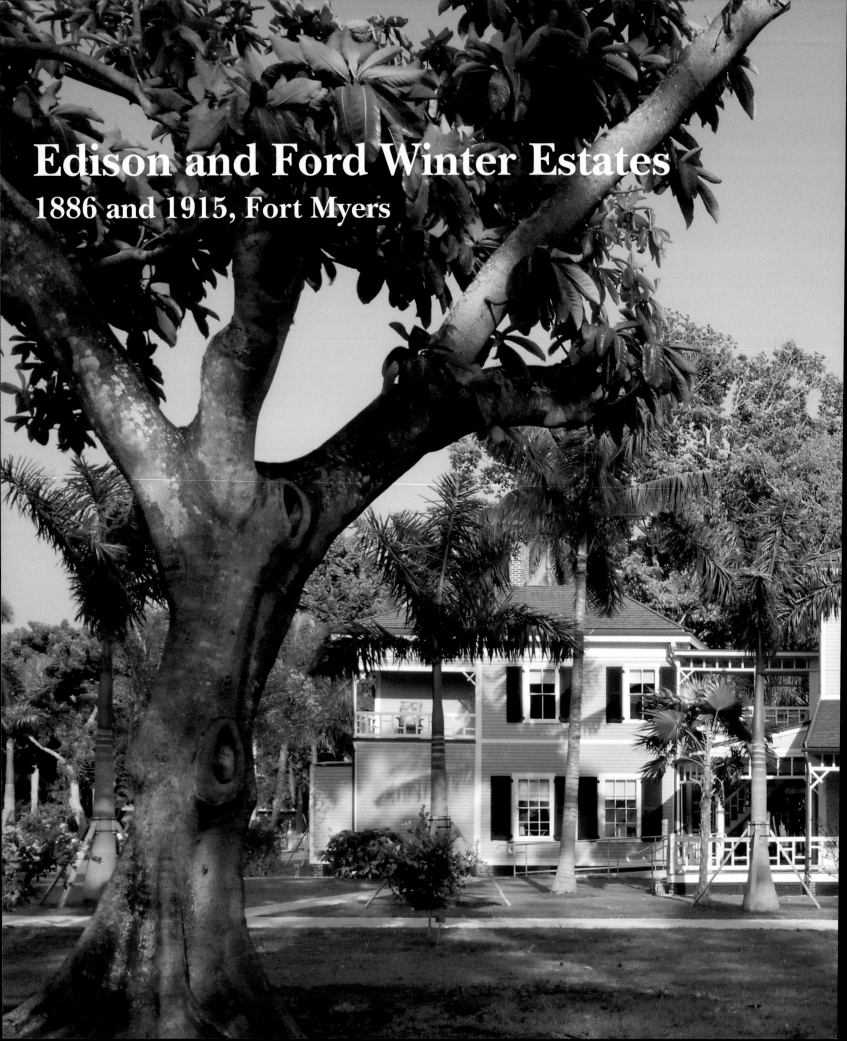

Edison and Ford Winter Estates
1886 and 1915, Fort Myers

PREVIOUS PAGES
A view of the Edison house, Seminole Lodge.

ABOVE
Thomas Edison's daughter, Madeleine, and friends formed a sewing circle on the veranda in 1912. Courtesy of the State Archives of Florida.

RIGHT
The living room had casual Bar Harbor–style wicker furniture. Mina Edison often played the George Steck piano. Edison designed and manufactured the "Electrolier" lighting fixtures in the early 1880s; fifteen are located throughout the estate.

I n 1885, seeking to find a botanical source for the filament of the light bulb, Thomas Edison explored the bamboo groves along the Caloosahatchee River and was inspired to purchase fourteen acres of riverfront land. Alden Frink, a Boston architect, reviewed and finalized Edison's sketches of the house of wood shipped from the Kennebec Framing Co. in Fairfield, Maine. In 1886, while Edison honeymooned nearby with his second wife, Mina Miller, Seminole Lodge was assembled. As the children were born—Madeleine (1888), Charles (1890), and Theodore (1898)—the house grew accordingly. In 1901, Edison used his own Edison Portland cement to build one of Florida's early inground pools, still a feature of the garden today.

The primary entrance to the estate was the riverfront. As in most of Florida, travel by water was faster and smoother than over land, and thus the major houses of this era faced the river. Soon, this would change. After

visiting Edison in Fort Myers in 1914, Henry Ford decided to purchase the neighboring property and in 1915 he built "The Mangoes." By this time the automobile entrance emerged as the new front door. Edison had already lined McGregor Boulevard with stately royal palms, a concept endorsed and ultimately extended into Fort Myers itself, and Ford used the grand boulevard to provide a front-yard drive through his groves.

The gardens of the properties were used for pleasure and science. Inspired by the rise in rubber prices during World War I, Edison, Ford, and their friend Harvey Firestone, founder of the Firestone Tire and Rubber Company, began the quest for a domestic source of rubber, forming the Edison Botanic Research Corporation in 1927. John Kunkel Small of the New York Botanical Garden, and a significant figure in Florida's botanical history,

assisted in plant collection and analysis, creating what University of Miami professor Rocco Ceo identifies as the "oldest and most significant experimental industrial botanical gardens in the United States." Far from the pressure of the company headquarters, yet fully outfitted with labs and testing grounds, the Florida homes presented an opportunity to retreat, but always with an eye to future opportunities.

In the 1920s, Ford established Greenfield Village near Detroit, assembling a collection of buildings important to the history of industrial America, including the 1886 Edison lab in Fort Myers. With Ford's funding, Edison replaced the lab with the "Little Office" and added the Moonlight Garden, which was planned by Clara Ford's landscape architect, Ellen Biddle Shipman, one of the leading designers of the era.

ABOVE
ABOVE
Henry Ford's estate, the Mangoes, was one of the first houses to face the river as well as the street, since Ford arrived in his Model T.

RIGHT
The Mangoes living room, with its casual wicker furniture, was the site of occasional square dances. Because Ford auctioned off the original furnishings, the room today has representative antiques and collectibles.

After Edison's death in 1931, the Fords began to shift their attention to "Richmond," the house that they had built on the site of the former Clay plantation near Savannah, along the Ogeechee River. Finally in 1945 Ford sold "The Mangoes" to the Thomas Biggar family. In February of 1947, Mrs. Edison donated the estate to the city of Fort Myers, and in November of that year, the house was opened to the public. Mrs. Edison died shortly thereafter, but the property continued to be a popular site.

In 1988, the city of Fort Myers purchased the Ford home from the Biggar family, and two years later, joined the two properties into a museum tour. Designated on the National Register of Historic Places in 1991, the properties are administered by the Thomas Edison and Henry Ford Winter Estates, Inc. Support from local philanthropy and the state of Florida funded restoration and renovation, which began in earnest in 2005 with extensive work on the buildings and gardens. The newly restored site brings to life the era of imagination and discovery that ultimately shaped the face of America today.

La Casita—Cigar Maker's House
1886, Tampa

T he Casitas, or "little houses," of the Ybor City Museum Park bring the nineteenth-century life of the cigar worker to Tampa's Ninth Avenue. Moved and reassembled into a streetscape, these three houses are among the first buildings erected in the Ybor City neighborhood. They are contemporary with the worker-housing movement, best known in the Pullman village in Illinois, where factory owners and manufacturers built small towns and villages in which the houses were leased or sold to the workers. Although the name Pullman eventually became synonymous with the strike against the company in 1894, the actual townscape was integrated into the neighboring city blocks, similar to the layout of Ybor City.

In Tampa, the arrival of Henry Plant's railroad in 1884 corresponds with the enhanced port facilities made possible by both the import of raw materials and the export of finished goods. By 1886, Don Vicente Martinez Ybor and Eduardo Manrara had identified an area east of Tampa for a settlement, and they set out to create a company town to support the work of the cigar trade, moving Ybor's Key West operation north.

By October 1886, Ybor and Manrara had amassed 111 acres in what became Ybor City, and another 1,000 acres east of Tampa. With the Ybor City Land and Improvement Company, the company provided basic infrastructure for water and waste, as well as support services, including police

PREVIOUS PAGES
The Casitas, or "little houses" of the local cigar-makers, date from roughly 1886 and are made of Florida pine with cedar-shingled roofs.

LEFT
The large portrait on the wall is of Dr. Jose Ramon Avellanal, who served as the director of the Centro Español mutual aid society. The other photographs are of the Marcos family, who owned a furniture business in Ybor and whose descendants donated several items to the historic site.

ABOVE
In this reconstruction of a working kitchen, the items are period but not original to the house, including the water pump in the foreground.

and firefighters. Both manufacturers and workers flocked to the area and Tampa quickly became known as the "Cigar Capital of the World," with more than two hundred cigar factories and workers from Cuba, Italy, and Spain.

The Casitas reflect adaptations of a model of building common to the coastal cities of the gulf, the "shotgun" house, a series of rooms that open directly one onto another without any hallway. Raised above the ground and a single room deep, with high ceilings and attic vents, the houses provided the necessary cross ventilation in the hot, humid environment.

Local pine, cypress, and cedar offered the Casitas protection from insects and humidity. In a less regimented operation than the towns of the industrial north, independent business provided retail, and workers were able to purchase the houses from factory owners through payroll-deduction plans. By the turn of the century, the city of Tampa had extended its infrastructure to the areas with sewers and indoor plumbing, and electricity quickly followed.

As the surrounding areas began to develop, preservationists realized the potential loss and moved rapidly to rescue the Casitas, as well as other neighborhood landmarks. Reassembled on Ninth Avenue, the Ybor City Museum Society opened the Centro Ybor Museum in the restored Centro Español club building to host exhibitions on the cigar industry as well as the greater life of the town. Today there are nine Casitas to explore and a streetscape that recalls the

Pinewood
1932, Lake Wales

PREVIOUS PAGES
Pinewood and its great lawn overlook the fragrant orange groves of Central Florida.

TOP
The entrance hall, with beamed ceiling and tile details, has doors made of cypress.

ABOVE
The planks of the hickory floor, along with the carpet and tapestry, give the living room warmth and character as a setting for concerts.

RIGHT
The loggia offers a view of a secluded courtyard through arched pocket doors.

Charles Austin Buck, vice president of Bethlehem Steel, began to plan the home that he called "El Retiro," known today as Pinewood, in 1930. The house was to be built on land within the 500-acre Mountain Lake Colony.

El Retiro commanded magnificent views of Edward Bok's new Sanctuary. Bok, former editor of *The Ladies' Home Journal,* and widely known for his Pulitzer Prize- winning autobiography, *The Americanization of Edward Bok,* began developing his ideas for the 157-acre Sanctuary in 1922, engaging Frederick Law Olmsted Jr., the planner

NEAR RIGHT
The steps from the morning room to the lower hall feature hand-painted Spanish tiles based on the floral and geometric patterns of Tunisia.

FAR RIGHT
Pinewood's lower hall features a seventeenth-century cardinal's chair and hand-painted Spanish tiles.

of Mountain Lake Colony and senior partner of the illustrious landscape firm Olmsted Brothers of Brookline, Massachusetts. The firm worked with Bok to create an oasis that would be "open and accessible to his friends and neighbors of the Mountain Lake Colony."

Olmsted recruited his former student and intern, landscape architect William Lyman Phillips, as the chief project designer from the Sanctuary's inception in 1924, through its completion in 1931. Phillips also directed the firm's work in the planning of Mountain Lake Colony, and designed many gardens for residents, often collaborating with Boston architect Charles R. Wait.

Buck, who decided to build a winter home in the colony after visiting his sister's place there, had worked in Cuba. He was eager to re-create the charm of the courtyard lifestyle of his Cuban home and found the climate of central Florida compatible with his intent. He discovered a sympathetic spirit, as well as incomparable expertise, in Phillips, who was well versed in tropical architecture and landscape after designing the town of Balboa in Panama in 1913.

From Phillips's perspective, the client and the topography permitted an opportunity to apply principles he had studied in the gardens of Europe. He began sketching the locations of major rooms and organizing axes for El Retiro's nearly eight acres, extending the major sight lines of the house to engage the beauty of the Sanctuary. Creating a composition in the manner of an Andalusian villa, Phillips opened the public rooms to expansive vistas and extended private rooms to enclosed courts and gardens.

As Phillips and Buck worked to establish the vision for El Retiro, Phillips wrote to Buck on June 5, 1929, to propose including an architect in the planning of the project because "the precise form taken by the house plan has so much bearing on the general plan for the grounds, and this particular problem presents so many possibilities for interesting adaptations to that site." Frustrated with the typical and hasty process of getting projects ready for owners, Phillips felt that "collaborative planning by owner, architect, and landscape architect" would lead to a "better, more interesting result." He offered to contact Wait, whom he believed was a very capable architect, and "more likely to take a liberal and cooperative attitude in problems of this sort than any of the other architects who are doing work at Mountain Lake."

The resulting project, with its highly integrated interior and exterior rooms and vistas, expresses the success of the team. Each room relates to a particular garden, terrace, court, or view. The "Bok Singing Tower," a carillon tower designed by Philadelphia architect Milton B. Medary and built in 1929, was featured as a prominent aspect from the main terrace of the house. Rising from the forest canopy, the marble and coquina tower draws the eye to the peak of Iron Mountain.

The design principles and vocabulary of El Retiro established a project that transcended time, a reality acknowledged in the listing of El Retiro in the National Register of Historic Places in 1985, and later as part of the landmark status awarded to the historic Bok Sanctuary in April 1993. Pinewood, the current name of the house, returns the villa to the origins of the site, a sandy eminence and home to a forest of native pines. As the early pines were supplemented with a forest and garden created by the Boks with the Olmsted team, and the house, created by Buck with Phillips and Wait, drew upon the first beauty of the site, the enhancements of artful design bring the visitor to a sense of place that is both local and universal.

Casa Feliz
1932, Winter Park

PREVIOUS PAGES
*James Gamble Rogers
Jr.'s 1932 masterpiece,
Casa Feliz, was moved
to its present-day
location approximately
seventy years after it was
built.*

ABOVE
*The library, which
borders on the loggia,
has its original random
oak flooring and, above
the fireplace, a painting
of Casa Feliz done by the
artist Don Sondag.*

RIGHT
*A sequence of archways
leads into the living
room.*

OPPOSITE
*The dramatic dining
room features timber-
frame ceilings.*

The architect of Casa Feliz, James Gamble Rogers II (1901–1990), was born into a family of architects. His father was John Arthur Rogers, who eventually—after working in the family's Chicago-based firm—moved to Daytona Beach. His distinguished uncle, James Gamble Rogers, famously designed Harkness Tower at Yale University, essentially creating what has become known as the "academic Gothic" style. In Florida, James Gamble Rogers II would become the foremost practitioner of what might be called the "Winter Park style"—an eclectic, deft-handed, Spanish-inspired Mediterranean architecture.

Casa Feliz, completed in 1932, is considered by many to be the most accomplished and elegant of all of Rogers's houses. It was designed for Robert Bruce Barbour and his wife, Nettie, who had first come to Winter Park in 1915. Robert Barbour was the owner of the Eclipse Chemical Engineering Company, a firm that made aniline dyes and indelible ink. Inspired by Rogers's own French-provincial-style home in Winter Park, Barbour then commissioned the architect to do a residence in the Spanish-Andalusian farmhouse style. The 5,400-square-foot house on the shore of Lake Osceola cost $25,000 to build.

The Barbour house was a center of cultural and social life in Winter Park, hosting Garden Club tours as well as concerts, meetings, poetry readings, and dinners. In 1938 and 1939 the Spanish Institute of Florida held a two-day fiesta at the Barbour house, and it was after these occasions that the house was renamed Casa Feliz.

The red-brick house has a plan that resembles a historically accurate version of an Andalusian *cortijo*, though according to Rogers's biographers Patrick W. and Debra McClane, the architecture of the house itself is better termed Spanish eclectic, as it draws on an array of

Mediterranean prototypes for its detailing. The house features deep, rounded arches as well as a single pointed arch over a passageway that divides the main house from the garage. The east facade boasts a shady loggia, while a heavy timber-columned balcony lines the second floor of the house's west facade.

In 2000, new owners of Casa Feliz determined they would demolish the house to make way for a larger residence. Preservation-minded members of the community responded by raising $1.2 million to move the house—it weighs 750 tons—across Interlachen Avenue to its current site on the Winter Park Golf Course. By use of Rogers's original blueprints and drawings as well as a set of 1937 photographs by Harold Haliday Costain, the house was painstakingly restored by craftsmen and is today under the auspices of the Winter Park Historical Society, open to visitors on Sunday afternoons and otherwise available for special functions, reflecting its long years as a focal point in the city's community life.

LEFT
The design of Casa Feliz was intended to be reminiscent of an Andalusian cortijo, but it is really more eclectic than definitive.

ABOVE
The courtyard is more specifically Andalusian with its herringbone brick paving and majolica-tile fountain.

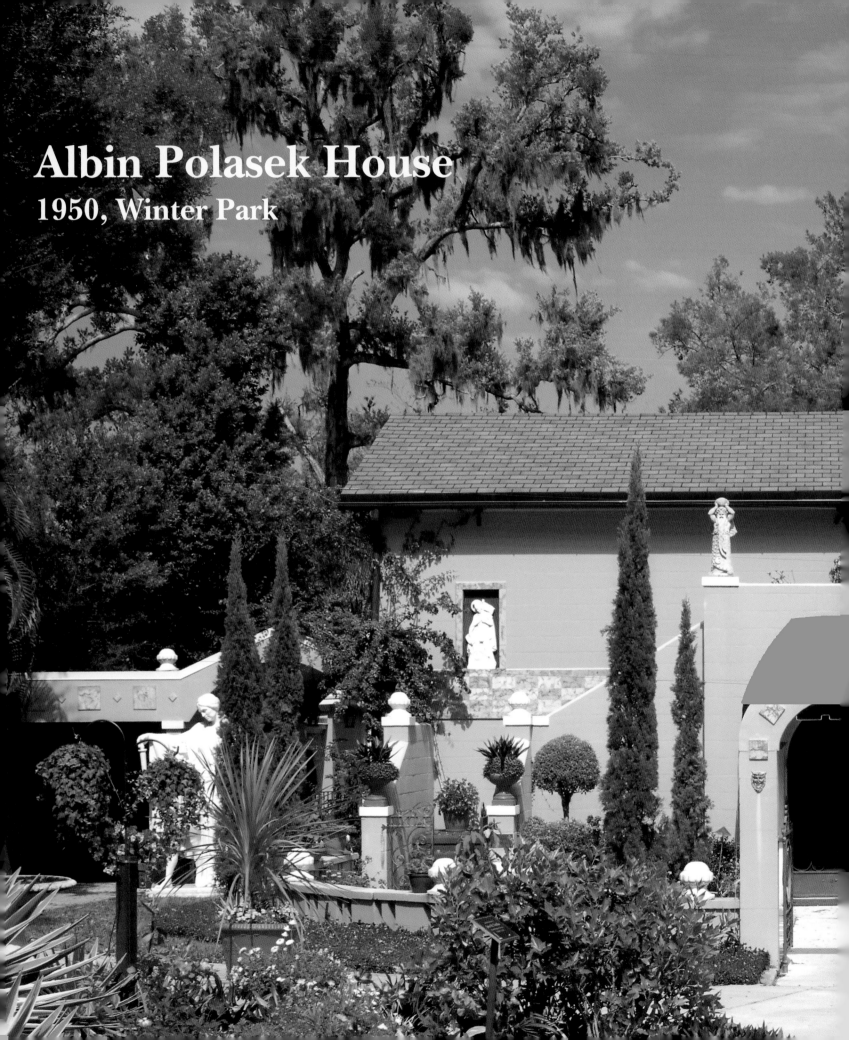

Albin Polasek House
1950, Winter Park

The story of this house is a bittersweet one. Albin Polasek, the sculptor who designed and built it, was paralyzed by a stroke just months after he moved in. The year was 1950. Confined to a wheelchair, he continued to paint, draw, work in clay, and carve in both wood and stone. He married twice, first to his longtime companion Ruth Sherwood, who died only eighteen months after their marriage, and subsequently, in 1961, at the age of eighty-two, to Emily Muska Kubat.

Polasek was born in Frenstat, Moravia, in what is now the Czech Republic. He immigrated to the United States at the age of twenty-two in 1901. Five years later, after working as a wood carver in the Midwest, he enrolled at the Pennsylvania Academy of Fine Arts. Soon his work was being recognized internationally, and he received a fellowship to study at the American Academy in Rome and an honorable mention at the 1913 Paris Salon. Eventually he became chairman of the department of sculpture at the Art Institute of Chicago and remained there for thirty years. It was during that time period that he was elected an associate member of the National Academy of Design.

His house in Winter Park was designed in the modified Spanish-Mediterranean style that is dominant in the Orlando suburb of Winter Park, an aesthetic established in part by the early architecture of Rollins College, including works by the Miami-based Richard Kiehnel as well as James Gamble Rogers Jr. The house has exaggerated rustic detailing and incorporates Spanish Colonial elements within a more traditional Mediterranean composition. Polasek was a devout Catholic, and the architecture and decoration of the house reflected the power of his spiritual convictions.

In 1961 the sculptor and his new wife established the Albin Polasek Foundation, setting about to buy back as many of his works as possible; eventually they were able to purchase approximately half, or two hundred of them. Many of the works are displayed within the house, which, with its large rooms, functions well as a museum; others are placed throughout the gardens.

PREVIOUS PAGES
The buildings of the Albin Polasek Museum and Sculpture Gardens reflect the architecture of the Mediterranean coast, but are painted in colors typical of Polasek's native Moravia with sculptures and tiles adorning the facade.

LEFT
The two-story salon of the residence features a Florida limestone fireplace. A portrait of Albin Polasek, painted by New England artist Charles W. Hawthorne, sits over the mantle.

155

TOP LEFT
Albin Polasek's bronze sculpture, Mother, *from 1927, stands at the street entrance. The work depicts a mother holding her younger child, while comforting the older one.*

BOTTOM LEFT
The unassuming entrance to the chapel is marked by distinct pink field tiles from Pennsylvania and a simple decorative bell. Polasek added the chapel to the property as a space for personal prayer and quiet reflection.

RIGHT
The Albin Polasek Museum and Sculpture Gardens welcomes visitors to the residence, chapel, gardens, and galleries of Czech-born American sculptor Albin Polasek. More than two hundred of the four hundred known works by Polasek are on the property, and regularly changing exhibits are offered in the museum's galleries.

Leu House
1888, Orlando

W hen Congress, in 1856, extended land grants to Florida's railroads and homesteaders, David W. Mizell was an immediate beneficiary, as he and his wife, Angeline, acquired the property of the present-day Leu House in 1858. John Thomas Mizell in 1888 built a farmhouse on his parents' land and in 1902, New Yorker Duncan Clarkston Pell acquired and expanded the property to plant an orange grove and build a winter retreat. Pell and his wife, Helen Louise Gardner, took the simple two-story wood-frame house and added to it, giving it such amenities as a library, a formal dining room, a detached kitchen, a master bedroom wing, and indoor plumbing, moving it well beyond its origins as a simple farmhouse. Pell's improvements attracted two new buyers, the Woodwards in 1906, and thirty years later, the Leus. As the role of the steam engine expanded, a young Harry P. Leu began to play an increasingly greater role in the Cain & O'Berry Boiler Co., eventually owning the company and

PREVIOUS PAGES
The Leu House started as a modest farmhouse but was expanded so that by 1906 it had acquired a certain quiet formality.

LEFT
The study, or library, has a few pieces of furniture from the Leu family as well as Harry Leu's book collection, trip souvenirs, and even the Leus' wedding invitation, framed on the long library table.

ABOVE
Furniture in the study includes a Martha Washington–style chair, c. 1930, that was part of the Leu family's collection.

transforming the boiler-repair enterprise into an extensive industrial-supply company with outlets in Miami and Tampa. Shortly after Leu married Mary Jane Schmidli, he acquired the forty-acre property. Drawing upon his own expertise and business interests, Leu introduced the latest electric and plumbing systems into the house while also developing the gardens. Particularly interested in exotic plants, the Leus traveled extensively to find material for the garden, likely influenced by the renowned gardens and collections of Dr. Henry Nehrling in nearby Gotha.

After an infusion of 240 varieties of camellias and an array of azaleas, the gardens of Leu House were opened to the public. After he retired from the company in the mid-1950s, Harry Leu joined his wife in the care of the property, finally deeding the house and gardens to the city of Orlando in 1961, "with the stipulation that it would always remain a botanical garden, nonprofit, and used for the sole purpose of the enjoyment and education of the public." The current house reveals the many layers of history of its individual owners, as well as the trajectory of this part of Florida from pine forest and flood plain into an economic engine that powered the railroads, and subsequently the state, into the modern era.

LEFT
The living room features a piano that was crafted in Vienna in 1858 (it is not original to the house). The furniture grouping next to the fireplace—including the lady's chair and piecrust table—was owned by the Leu family.

ABOVE
The living room is part of the original house, which was expanded by the Pell family in 1889, giving the house its current two-story configuration.

TOP
A shady grove in the Leu gardens where Spanish moss covers the trees.

ABOVE
The garden clock was given to the Leu House Museum by a local Kiwanis Club in the 1970s. The clock has a diameter of forty feet and the Roman numerals are two-and-a-half feet high.

RIGHT
The rose garden is now located where historically a grapefruit grove was planted. An earlier rose garden was situated nearer to the lake.

Withers-Maguire House

1888, Ocoee

PREVIOUS PAGES
*The gabled wood-frame
Withers-Maguire House
was originally built on
eight acres in what was
then the rural town of
Ocoee.*

ABOVE
*The piano, which
originally belonged to
a local music teacher,
was donated to the Leu
House Museum by the
Ocoee Christian Church.*

RIGHT
*For many years, the
woodwork throughout
the house was painted,
but during restoration
it was determined that
the wood was originally
unpainted. The rugs
in the living room
were found rolled up
underneath the house.*

Confederate Brigadier General William
Temple Withers, an attorney and horse breeder, moved to
Florida in the late 1880s to recuperate from a musket-ball
wound in a milder climate than his Kentucky home
afforded him. He chose the Central Florida town of
Ocoee on the shores of Lake Apopka. Ocoee had first
been settled by Dr. D. J. Starke who brought with him a
group of slaves all of whom, including himself, were suf-
fering from malaria. Starke hoped—successfully—that
the cleaner water and better living conditions would be
salubrious. He named the settlement Starke Lake.

It was not until after the Civil War that the area was
permanently settled, when Captain Buford Sims of Tennessee moved there to plant Florida's first citrus groves.
The town was platted in 1865 and the name changed to
Ocoee. By the time Withers arrived, the town was well
established, sending oranges and winter crops north via
the Florida Midland Railroad. Withers had traveled to St.
Augustine where he met Buford Sims, who, in turn,

OPPOSITE
*"Miss Lillian's Room"
is so named in honor
of Lillian Maguire who
graduated in 1918 from
Florida State College for
Women, and later
received a master's
degree from Columbia
University. She taught
at a college in Kansas
until her mother's ill
health caused her to
return home, after which
she taught at the
University of Florida.
The room represents
her life in 1918.*

TOP
*The dining set is in the
Empire-revival style and
was purchased from a
house in Charleston,
South Carolina.*

ABOVE
*The kitchen was
originally a pantry. It
currently features such
oddities as an electrified
butter churn and a
bottle capper.*

encouraged the Kentuckian to move to his town of Ocoee; Withers followed with his wife, Martha, and four of their eight children, building his house on nine acres there in 1888. Along with a gabled wooden-frame house, he built a boat house, a chicken coop, and a barn; the entire project cost $3,700. The house, typical of its era, had stick-style architectural elements with a double-story veranda on its south facade and single-story verandas on the east and west sides.

Withers was not to live in it long. However, by the time he died in 1889, he had established the Christian Church in Ocoee, this after holding services in his living room and sending a carriage each Sunday to Orlando—some thirteen miles to the east—to bring the minister to preach. Although he donated the money to build the church, he did not live to see it completed. The house remained in the Withers family—Martha Withers lived there in the winters and three of the Withers's daughters remained on year-round until they married. In 1910, David O. Maguire purchased it.

Maguire was from Gwinnet County, Georgia, where his family had experienced General Sherman's march through the state. Faced with the difficulties of recovery, five of the Maguire siblings (two brothers, including David, and three sisters) moved to Central Florida, at first settling on Lake Apopka and later near Ocoee, where they became involved in the flourishing citrus and other agricultural industries. When David Maguire's house burned in 1910, he offered to buy the Withers house and its furnishings. His offer of $5,000 was paid out in $1,000-a-year increments.

That he purchased the furniture was a stroke of historical luck in that much of what can be seen today is original to the Withers-Maguire house. The Maguire family lived in the house for seventy-three years. In 1984, the city of Ocoee was able to acquire the house and restored it, ultimately creating the house museum that exists today.

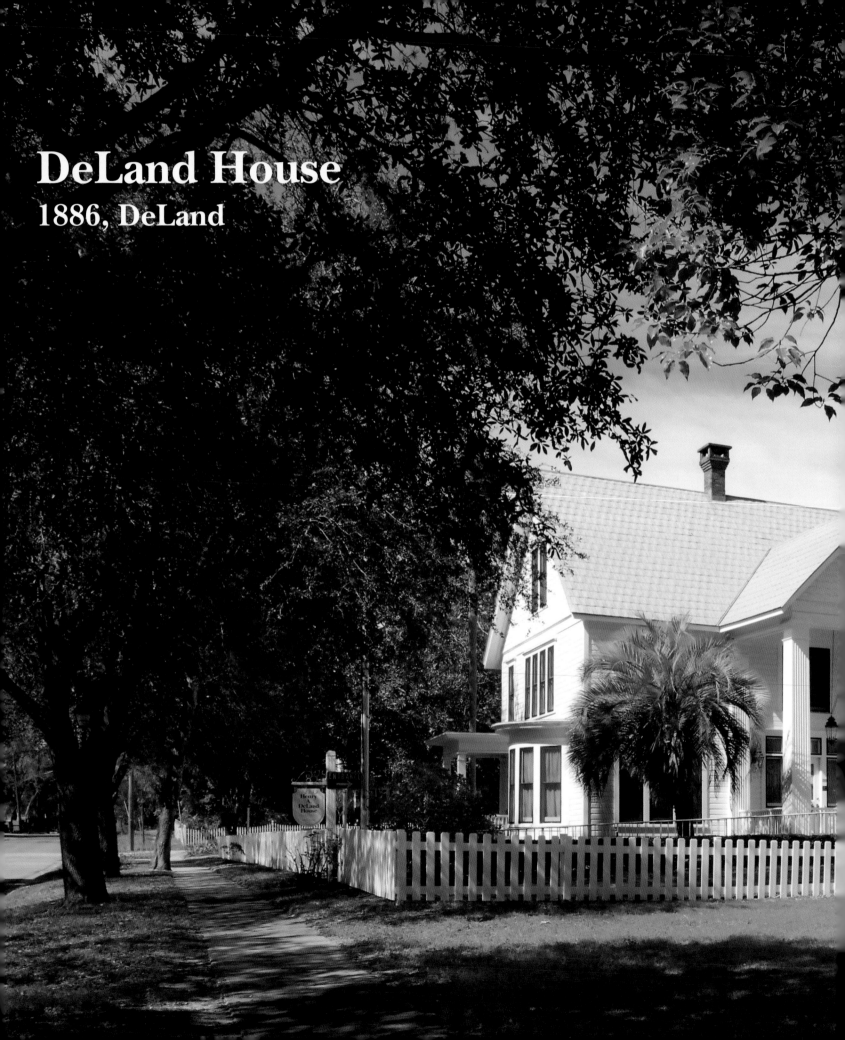

DeLand House
1886, DeLand

PREVIOUS PAGES
*Front view of the
DeLand House
Museum.*

FAR LEFT
*The formal front parlor
of the DeLand House.*

NEAR LEFT
*The oil painting depicts
Dr. Charles Farriss,
professor of Greek, vice
president of Stetson
University, and owner
of the house from 1903
to 1935.*

S urviving the era of urban renewal with grace and charm intact, the city of DeLand offers a window into Florida's past. Every aspect of the story is here: boom, bust, period architecture and eccentric villas, millionaires and hardworking locals, and all the diverse groups of people who keep the landscape in check, the buildings maintained, and life stable. Within the general context of historic DeLand, four houses represent the threads of its history. The DeLand House reveals the transformation from Victorian to neoclassical architecture that was occurring in the region. The Stetson Mansion represents the grand vision of a powerful owner. The President's House at Stetson University offers a counterpoint in its staid architecture, which gives it iconic value to the institution, while the DeBary House, just outside

the town illustrates the root of the town's original architectural vocabulary. Each is significant to the overall story of DeLand's history.

In 1876, Henry DeLand, planning to retire from his career manufacturing baking powder in New York, acquired land near the town of Spring Hill. Appreciating the success of his citrus crop as well as the benefits of Florida's climate, DeLand sold acreage with guaranteed money back, a promise that he honored, and in 1882 the city of DeLand was incorporated. Four years later Henry DeLand, faced with a financial crisis when he bought back properties from investors after a freeze destroyed the citrus crops, returned to his New York company. John Stetson, the Philadelphian hat manufacturer, arrived to build his estate and lend support to the town.

The DeLand House brings the era of Victorian Florida to life. Donated by Robert and Hawtense Conrad, with period furnishings and artifacts provided by the citizens of DeLand, the DeLand House Museum opened to the public in 1990. Currently home of the West Volusia County Historical Society, the Robert M. Conrad Educational Research Center, and the Lue Gim Gong Memorial Garden, the DeLand House was originally built, within an orange grove, in 1886 for Henry DeLand's attorney, Arthur George Hamlin. Just seven years later, John B. Stetson bought the residence for faculty housing, and by 1903, Dr. Charles Farriss, professor of Greek, purchased it and transformed the dimensions and details of the house, culminating in the addition of a Greek-Revival portico on the east elevation.

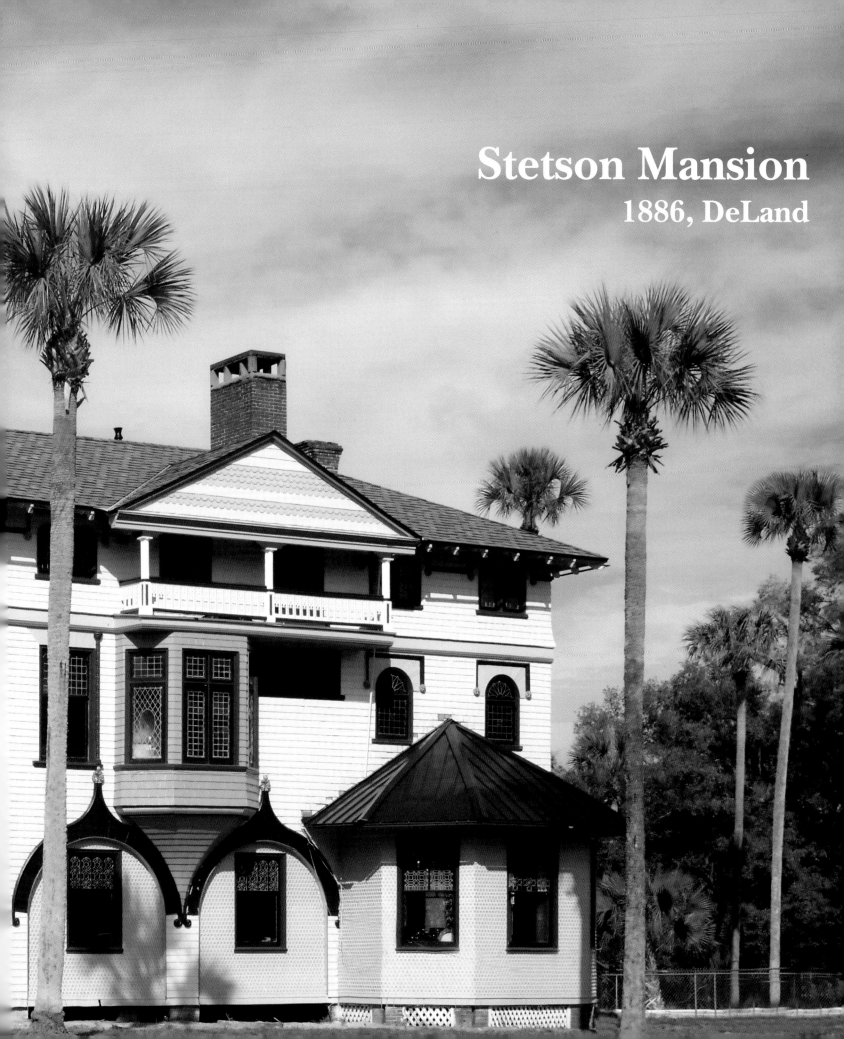

Stetson Mansion
1886, DeLand

PREVIOUS PAGES
Having an eclectic blend of architectural styles, the 1886 residence of John B. Stetson embodies the lively energy of its time.

NEAR RIGHT
With more than 10,000 panes of leaded glass, each room features a unique pattern both in the windows and in the parquet work of the floors.

FAR RIGHT
Using imported woods, the paneling, lattice, floors, and balustrades were milled directly on the site.

FOLLOWING PAGES
The view across the reception parlor extends to the adjoining music room and library.

J ohn B. Stetson engaged the architect George T. Pearson to develop plans for an estate that expressed the exuberance of the era. Orchestrating Gothic, Tudor, Moorish, and Polynesian details into the composition, the 10,000-square-foot house features inlaid parquet floors, stained-glass windows with roundels, and many interior embellishments. On the two-acre property, a schoolhouse was built for the Stetson children. Stetson donated generously to DeLand University, which was renamed in 1889 the John B. Stetson University.

Listed in the National Register of Historic Places since 1978, the Stetson Mansion's restoration began in earnest in 2006, with the exterior of the house completed as shown here.

Stetson University
President's House
1910, DeLand

PREVIOUS PAGES
Four imposing columns mark the double veranda of the former Steed House built in 1910.

LEFT
The house features antiques collected by former Stetson University President Dr. Howard Lee and Mrs. Lee. Dr. Lee's father made both the Williamsburg-style desk and grandfather clock. The art is all from the Lee family's personal collection.

In 1948, Stetson University acquired the 1910 residence that was built for W. A. Steed. An example of turn-of-the century neoclassicism, the house exemplified the classical tradition that inspired the university's own curriculum. The President's House extends out to gardens and pavilions that recall the larger estate of the Steed era. The newest addition to the house, the Vera Lea Rinker Native Plant Garden, reintroduces plant materials that would have been seen in DeLand's early days.

ABOVE
The dining room is used for formal entertaining.

FOLLOWING PAGES
The back porch and native-plant garden offer a spot for more casual gatherings.

187

DeBary Hall
1870, DeLand

PREVIOUS PAGES
DeBary Hall dates from the early 1870s, when New York wine merchant Frederick deBary bought land near the St. Johns River for a winter retreat.

RIGHT
Today, DeBary Hall features family portraits that originally hung in the deBarys's New York homes. (Originally, this Florida retreat had paintings of European landscapes and rural life, but estate sales scattered them years ago.)

BELOW
The dining room's current furnishings, while period, are not original to the house.

BELOW
An 1895 photograph shows an unidentified group gathered on the porch of DeBary Hall. Courtesy of the State Archives of Florida.

OPPOSITE
The parlor features a nineteenth-century square piano.

Built in 1870 as a winter retreat near Lake Monroe, DeBary Hall occupied a 6,000-acre property with orange groves, gardens, and outbuildings. Frederick deBary, a wine importer and salesman in New York, also operated the DeBary-Baya Merchant's Line, a commercial steamboating venture along the St. Johns River. Visitors and tourists enjoyed hunting and fishing in the pinelands of the vast estate. Enlarged a decade later, both stories of DeBary Hall have wraparound verandas backed by tall windows looking out to the landscaped grounds, a decorative fountain, orange groves, and the path to a spring-fed swimming pool. The current historic site occupies about ten acres and includes the 8,000-square-foot main house, several outbuildings, and artifacts of DeBary Hall's agricultural past.

Marjorie Kinnan Rawlings House
c. 1880s, Cross Creek

PREVIOUS PAGES
The back of the Rawlings house can be seen over the seasonal garden. Planted twice a year, in the spring and fall, the garden has herbs, flowers, and vegetables.

ABOVE RIGHT
Marjorie Kinnan Rawlings (c. 1940), shown here with the typewriter she used at Cross Creek, did much of her writing outdoors. Courtesy of the State Archives of Florida.

FAR RIGHT
The living room was further opened up to the Florida light when Rawlings took out a wall dividing the original cabin and put in French-style glass windows and doors along the east wall. The fireplace, which is still functional, provided the only heat.

T he Pulitzer Prize-winning author whose captivating novel, *The Yearling,* has kept generations of readers spellbound, lived most simply in a frame house set in the woodlands of North Central Florida. Marjorie Kinnan Rawlings lived in this house from 1928 to 1941, and it was during this time that she wrote prolifically of the people and the place, vividly depicting both.

Born in 1896 in Washington D.C., Rawlings graduated from the University of Wisconsin and then moved to New York, where she soon married her college classmate and fellow aspiring writer, Charles Rawlings. They moved first to Louisville, Kentucky, and then to Rochester, New York, to work as newspaper writers. While still a columnist for a Rochester, New York, newspaper, Rawlings used an inheritance from her mother to buy seventy-four acres of orange groves in a remote spot between Gainesville and Ocala. She sought a rural location to pursue her writing and, further, to deal with her troubled marriage.

Soon it was not the remoteness that empowered her writing but her immediate attachment to the landscape and her connections to the people of Cross Creek and the Central Florida landscape. Rawlings's first novel, *South Moon Under,* brought attention not just to her (the book was a selection of the Book-of-the-Month Club and a Pulitzer Prize finalist), but also to the little hamlet of Cross Creek. It was *The Yearling* that catapulted her to fame, including the 1939 Pulitzer Prize for fiction and membership in the National Academy of Arts and Letters. She had been divorced in 1933 and was remarried in 1941, this time to hotelier Charles Baskin. With him, she moved to St. Augustine; even though Rawlings also owned

a cottage in Crescent Beach, Florida, and a farmhouse in Van Hornesville, New York, she frequently returned to Cross Creek.

The house itself dates back to the 1880s but was added to over the years. It sits "snugly," as Rawlings said in her memoir *Cross Creek*, under the orange trees with "a simple grace of line, low rambling, and one-storied." Typical of the cracker style (ubiquitously found in Northern and Central Florida, as well as in rural Georgia and elsewhere in the south), the house is an L-shape structure with porches and ample overhangs set back from a two-lane country road. Rawlings did much of her writing from the screened front porch.

The house and farmyard on five acres of land are a National Historic Site within the Florida State Parks system; the property is at once a testimony to the spare pioneer life, and even more so to the ethic of living in concert with the land. Memorably, Rawlings wrote at the end of *Cross Creek*: "It seems to me that the earth may be borrowed but not bought. It may be used but not owned. We are tenants, not possessors; lovers, and not masters."

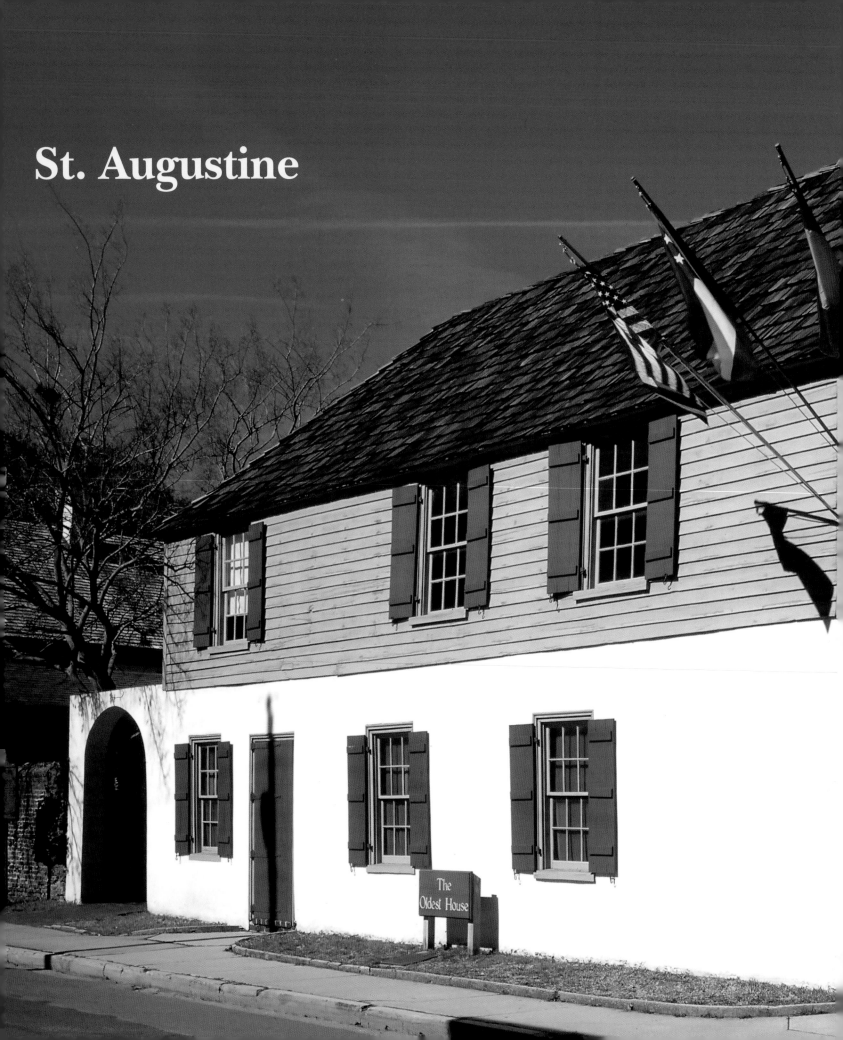

St. Augustine

González-Alvarez House
1700s

PREVIOUS PAGES
The González-Alvarez House sports the flags of the countries that ruled over St. Augustine. The original house was a two-room coquina-rock structure, which belonged to the Tomas González family. In 1763, when the Spanish turned over the rule of the city, British Major Joseph Peavett took over the house and enlarged it to its current size. Then in 1790, a Spaniard named Geronimo Alvarez bought it at auction. His descendants occupied it for the next one hundred years.

S t. Augustine's past is storied. In 1513 as he sailed up the coastline, Don Juan Ponce de León claimed it for Spain. He named it La Florida, which for the following fifty years was an ironic euphemism as the Spanish tried and failed to settle the "Land of Flowers." The first settlement along the Atlantic coast came in 1564 when the French built a fort on the St. Johns River. In turn, Admiral Don Pedro Menéndez de Avilés was named as Florida's first governor, with orders to colonize the area. He arrived in 1565 at the Timucuan Indian village called Seloy, immediately fortifying and renaming it St. Augustine. St. Augustine remained under Spanish rule (weathering attacks from Sir Francis Drake, Sir James Moore, and James Oglethorpe) until the 1763 Treaty of Paris, when it was ceded to Great Britain; that was to last twenty years until 1783 when Florida was returned to Spain, a rule that lasted until the United States bought and colonized it in 1821. Difficult years—of yellow-fever epidemics and the Seminole Wars—were to follow, with prosperity only intermittent.

OPPOSITE
A re-creation of a typical British tavern

TOP
"Maria's Room" is restored to the British era, and typical of the time, it did double duty as both a dining room and bedroom.

ABOVE
Period furniture, objects, and clothing depict eighteenth-century life.

Ximénez-Fatio House
1798

ABOVE

In approximately 1798, the merchant Andres Ximenez built a two-story coquina blockhouse with two warehouses and a kitchen building. By the early nineteenth century, the owners of the house were Margaret and Samuel Cook. After Samuel's death in 1826, Margaret turned

the capacious residence into a boarding house, which ultimately—after another change of owners—was operated by the very popular Miss Louisa Fatio.

RIGHT

The owner's parlor was kept private from the guests. An astral lamp lit the room at night.

Indeed it was not until the oil and railroad magnate Henry Flagler arrived there in 1885 that the town began to flourish. Flagler was to build a number of significant structures, most notably two grand hotels—the Ponce de León (now Flagler College) and the Alcazar—with the then-fledgling architectural firm of Carrère & Hastings, which brought to St. Augustine a narrative architectural style that imparted the fictive idea of past Spanish grandeur.

Even before Flagler came to town, a group of local residents had begun meeting to form the St. Augustine Historical Society, which was formally inaugurated in 1883. The first purchase was a colonial house known as the Vedder Museum, but it was lost completely in a fire in 1914. Four years later, the society purchased two houses, the Tovar House and the González-Alvarez House, the oldest surviving house in St. Augustine, which dates to 1706. Today the society also operates a museum and the Fernández-Llambias House.

It was not until 1959 that the state of Florida began earnest efforts to preserve St. Augustine's earliest architectural heritage. Today, St. Augustine's historic buildings (many of which are reconstructions of originals) encompass an almost two-century time span from 1703 to 1898. Notable among these is the Ximénez-Fatio House, which dates to 1798 and was built by the Spanish-born Andrés Ximénez of coquina rock with tabby stone floors. He operated a general store on the ground floor and the family lived above; their tenancy, however, was short-lived, as by

LEFT
The Ximénez-Fatio House, in its former days as a boarding house and inn, welcomed travelers to early St. Augustine. Guests took repast in this ample dining room, which was fitted with fringed ceiling fans.

ABOVE
The kitchen was located in a separate building behind the house and had a broad fireplace as well as a bake oven. It is the only original eighteenth-century freestanding kitchen in St. Augustine.

Peña-Peck House
1750

1806 the entire young family of seven had died. In 1826, Margaret Cook—who had arrived from Charleston with her husband, Samuel—bought the house, and it became a boarding house that attracted early tourists at first, then soldiers who billeted there during the Seminole Wars, followed quickly by refugees whose plantations had been burned.

Louisa Fatio operated the inn for five years, starting in 1850, and then bought it five years later. Her heirs sold it to the National Society of the Colonial Dames of America in the State of Florida in 1939, and the Ximénez-Fatio House is now run as a museum depicting early tourism in St. Augustine.

Also noteworthy is the Peña-Peck House, which was built of native coquina stone in 1750 as the home of the Spanish royal treasurer Juan Estéban de Peña. During the British period it became home to the colonial lieutenant governor, Sir John Moultrie, who had come from Charleston, South Carolina. It later became the home of Dr. Seth Peck and his family. Peck had arrived in St. Augustine with his wife, Sarah, and their five children in 1833. In 1837, he purchased the house and added a second story. In 1933, a century later, the last surviving member of the Peck family, Anna Gardner Burt, donated it to the city of St. Augustine. Today, it is operated as a house museum by the Women's Exchange.

Goodwood
c. 1830s, Tallahassee

PREVIOUS PAGES
The exterior of the main house at Goodwood.

ABOVE
The dining room of the main house features the original marble fireplace.

OPPOSITE
The north, or back, parlor at Goodwood has one of two of the house's frescoed ceilings, the oldest in Florida.

History has touched Goodwood in tragic, beautiful, and later, happier ways. First established in 1832 when Hardy Bryan Croom and his wife, Frances Smith, left North Carolina, the 2,400-acre parcel was located three miles from Tallahassee, then the capital of the territory. It was well positioned for, as his descendant John Croom wrote more than a hundred years later, "good society, pleasantly situated on the border of Lake Lafayette, and combining many advantages for a permanent family seat."

The house that Hardy Croom erected exemplifies the plantation architecture of its era and featured some of Florida's first frescoes. It was one of two plantation houses that Croom built, the second sited on the west bank of the Apalachicola River near Marianna. Croom's notable discovery of a rare conifer occurred as he traveled from one to the other. He named the tree *Toreya taxifolium* after his colleague and friend, the New York botanist, Dr. John Torrey, who subsequently returned the favor, naming the delicate and rare Florida wildflower *Croomia pauciflora*.

Croom, his wife, and three children were lost in the wreck of the steamship *Home* in 1837. Croom's brother Bryan and his wife, Evelina—the granddaughter of John Hawks, the architect sent to the North Carolina colony by King George III to design the Tryon Palace in New Bern—then occupied the property. Frances Smith Croom's mother and sister, as beneficiaries of the Croom children, successfully sued the Croom family for possession of the plantations, and after the Florida Supreme Court decision in 1857, Frances Smith Croom's niece, Susan Armistead Winthrop, acquired the property. Arvah Hopkins, the next owner, held the property throughout the Civil War and sold it upon her husband's death in 1885. Dr. William Lamb Arrowsmith and his wife, Elizabeth,

PREVIOUS PAGES
The south, or front, parlor features an elaborate frescoed ceiling and a carved marble fireplace.

ABOVE
The master bedroom includes the bed used by Bryan Croom, owner of Goodwood from 1837 to 1857.

RIGHT
The southwest bedroom used by the last mistress of Goodwood, Margaret Hodges Hood, from 1925 until her death in 1978.

acquired the now-160-acre estate. After her husband's death, Elizabeth Arrowsmith remained in the house for twenty-five years, finally selling Goodwood to Fanny Tiers, widow of Alexander Tiers, of Farmlands, in Morris County, New Jersey.

Curators at Goodwood today attribute the current condition of the estate to the work of Fanny Tiers (whose daughter Esther married Bache Hamilton Brown; Brown, a graduate of the architecture program at Columbia University, was best known for his introduction of the Luxor fishing reel). The Tiers family wintered at Goodwood until 1925, when Fanny Tiers sold Goodwood to State Senator William C. Hodges and his wife, Margaret. Once again Goodwood resumed a central role in Tallahassee society, even after the senator's death in 1940. When the remarried Margaret Hodges died in 1978, her widower, Thomas M. Hood, established the Margaret E. Wilson Foundation, which upon his death in 1990, assumed stewardship of Goodwood.

The interiors of the house are original. The garden has been restored, using plants that predate 1929, the era of the garden's second restoration, contributing to regional resources for heirloom plants.

Knott House
1843, Tallahassee

NEAR AND FAR RIGHT
*The house was restored
to a 1928 date with all
the original belongings
of Mr. and Mrs.
William Valentine
Knott. These rooms were
used for entertaining,
music, and civic
endeavors. Luella Pugh
Knott had the wall
removed between the two
parlors to form one large
library with Victorian
and Renaissance-revival
furnishings. Mrs. Knott
avidly wrote poetry and
attached her poems to
the furniture with satin
ribbons. Some of them
served as lyrics to music
she wrote, which she
played on the Weber
piano. Antique mirrors
enhance the grandeur
and light.*

The 1843 Knott House holds a singular distinction in that it is thought to have been built by George Proctor, a free black builder. Some twenty-two years later, in 1865, the house became the temporary headquarters of the occupying Union Army, and General Edward M. McCook of the army read the Emancipation Proclamation from the front steps, officially announcing the end of slavery. Intriguingly, though its owners were all white, the house's early history continued to be tied up with civil-rights history, when the second owner, a physician named George Betton, sponsored the medical training of the first African-American to graduate from medical school.

The first occupants were a Tallahassee attorney, Thomas Hagner, and his wife, Catherine Gamble Hagner. Approximately ten years after they moved in, the Hagners doubled the size of the house, from six to twelve rooms. In 1883, Catherine Hagner sold the house to

ABOVE
*A Victor radio and an
Electrola gramophone
provided the Knotts with
entertainment and
information.*

RIGHT
*The crystal chandelier
positioned in front of the
mirror in the dining
room created an inviting
setting for tea parties or
dinners with political
dignitaries.*

FOLLOWING PAGES
*William Knott was
considered a judicious
man and spoke about
many social issues and
concerns. He rested in
his bedroom on the
second floor of the house
in his imposing
Renaissance-revival
half-tester bed.*

Dr. Betton. Subsequently, three Florida Supreme Court justices and their families lived in the Knott House one after another.

In 1928, the house was purchased by William Valentine Knott and Luella Pugh Knott, and it was shortly after the purchase that Luella Knott added the grand classical-revival portico to the front of the building. An orphan who had made her way through Greensboro Methodist College in North Carolina, Luella Knott became a schoolteacher in Central Florida, where she met and married William, whose political aspirations were to take them to Tallahassee. The Knott family had moved by covered wagon from Florida to Georgia in 1881 to establish citrus groves and later mine phosphates, but William's interests veered elsewhere. By 1897, he had become the state's first financial agent, and by 1901 he had become the first state auditor and subsequently state treasurer and comptroller. After a stint away from Tallahassee following a failed gubernatorial campaign, the Knotts moved back when William was appointed, for a second time, state auditor and then state treasurer, a post he held from 1928 to 1941.

The Knotts filled their house with Victorian furniture, much of which Luella Knott found at estate sales. The three Knott children were educated at home, and Luella was known for the poems she wrote and attached to furniture and objects around the house. After William and Luella's deaths in 1965, their son J. Charles Knott inherited it. The family lived in the house until 1985, when it was given to the Historic Tallahassee Preservation Board.

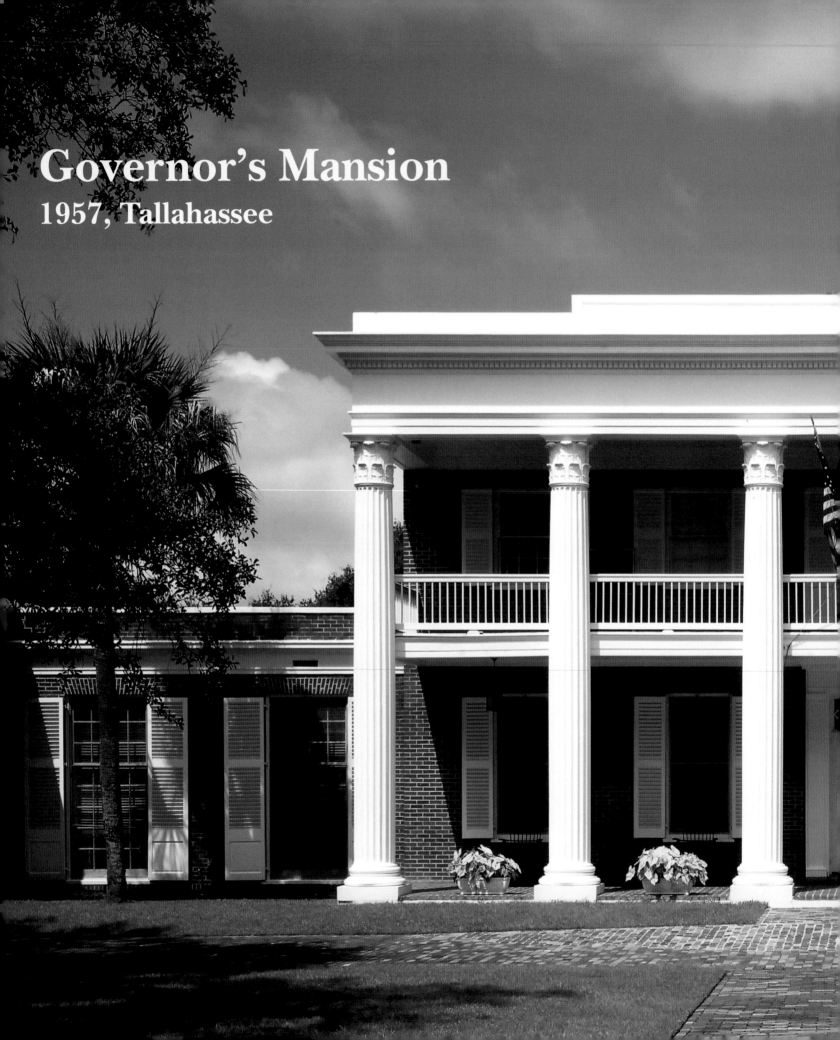

Governor's Mansion

1957, Tallahassee

PREVIOUS PAGES
*The Florida Governor's
Mansion long occupied
this site, but the current
house was begun in
1955 and was
completed in 1957.*

NEAR AND FAR RIGHT
*The State Reception
Room is seen by
thousands of visitors
each year. The room
reflects the delicate
architectural hand of
Marion Syms Wyeth
and the decorative
finesse of James Cogar.*

T he Florida Governor's Mansion is the second house to occupy the same site. It was built in 1957
and designed by the fine Palm Beach architect Marion
Syms Wyeth late in his career. Previously on the site was a
1907 house that had been occupied by eleven governors.
However, in 1955, the original Governor's Mansion was
determined to be structurally unsound and thus was
demolished.

Wyeth's new Governor's Mansion was based, in part,
on the Hermitage, the Tennessee home of President
Andrew Jackson from 1804 until his death in 1845. The
house was completed in 1821 and enlarged by the
Nashville, Tennessee, architect David Morrison starting
in 1831 during Jackson's presidency. It was this latter
intervention—the addition of a two-story entrance portico with Doric columns—that provided the starting point
for Wyeth's design. Appropriately and symbolically,

Andrew Jackson had been Florida's first territorial governor. A portrait of Jackson hangs in the mansion's state guest bedroom.

An elegant and versatile architect, the long-lived Wyeth (1889–1982) left his job at Carrère & Hastings in New York in 1919 and moved to Palm Beach just at the beginning of the town's great boom. In its heyday, his firm (Wyeth, King & Johnson and later Wyeth and King) had offices in both Palm Beach and New York, and their work received national attention and honors. Wyeth designed in the Mediterranean and other European-inspired styles— including the Andalusian influenced Cielito Lindo—in Palm Beach and created the Dutch South African Village in Coral Gables, Florida. His 1941 Norton Museum of Art in West Palm Beach fuses Art Deco and neoclassical elements; the Norton residence, however, was designed in the Monterey style.

For the Governor's Mansion, Wyeth opted for the neoclassical style. Like the Hermitage, it is red brick with a tall portico; however, the columns are Corinthian, rather than the Doric order used in Jackson's house. Inside, the house is divided into public and private parishes, with the southern end of the main floor and the second floor belonging to the family and the rest of the house devoted to the public, with reception spaces and state rooms.

The Kentucky-born James Cogar (1906–1987), the first curator of Colonial Williamsburg and an expert on European and American antiques (he had previously curated the furnishings for the Palace of the Governors of Virginia), was selected as the mansion's interior designer. He opted for a formal but accessible colonial style and traveled to England, Scotland, and Ireland to locate eighteenth- and nineteenth-century furniture for the mansion. He wrote at the time that "My overall plan for the Governor's Mansion would be to have it a dignified interior, painted in a harmonious color scheme, furnished in good taste with pieces of character, and although an official residence, give to it the feeling that it is a gracious home of quiet beauty that would please but not overpower those that are entertained there."

LEFT
The dining room is quite versatile. Guests can be seated at the long table shown here, or it can be replaced by six round tables that can seat up to fifty people. The silver service was purchased in 1911 by the people of the state of Florida as a gift to the USS Florida. When the ship was decommissioned in 1930, the set was returned to the Governor's Mansion.

231

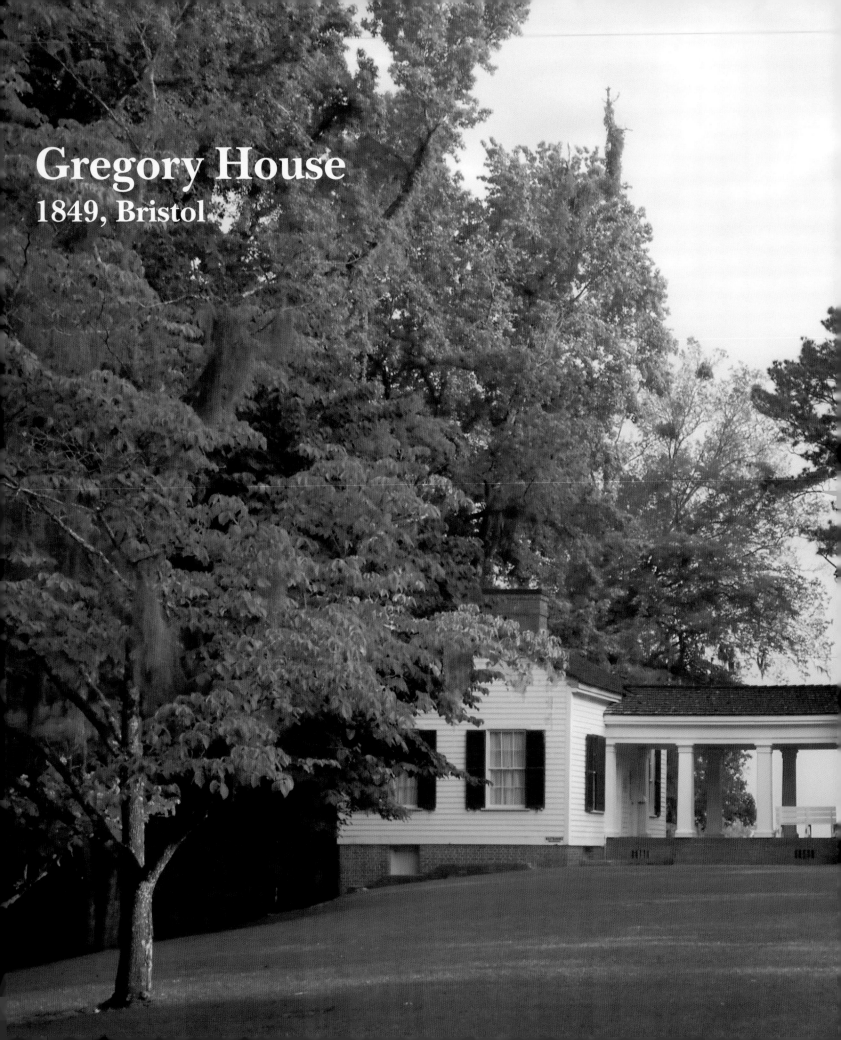

Gregory House
1849, Bristol

I n the mid-nineteenth century, Jason Gregory was among the most prosperous and active planters along the Apalachicola River. He had, over the years, been able to purchase almost all of the lots in the town of Ocheesee along with some 3,600 acres of farmland. In 1849 he built a commanding house with one Federal-style facade and the other classical revival.

Between the years of 1850 and 1865, the Gregory House was a major social center in Calhoun County as it was located at a midway stopping point—then called Ocheesee Landing—between Columbus, Georgia, and Apalachicola. The house became an oasis for many important dignitaries—politicians, elected officials, jurists, and others. However, after the end of the Civil War, Calhoun County became increasingly less prosperous. Gregory's fortunes, dependent on slavery, faltered completely. The Gregory plantation house was occupied intermittently, but eventually it was abandoned and stood empty.

PREVIOUS PAGES
The rear facade of the Gregory House with the kitchen on the left, separated from the main house by a breezeway.

LEFT
A highlight of the parlor is the spectacular rosewood mid-nineteenth-century J. Pirsson piano.

ABOVE
The plantation office holds pieces reflecting the art of candle making, and a beautiful gentleman's desk with a fold-down writing area.

A memoir of Callie Scott McClellan shows that the McClellans lived in the house for a period in 1919. Callie had in 1915 married the widower Jessie McClellan, who traveled through the Florida Panhandle as a paymaster and operator of commissaries, among other business endeavors. While living in the house, she reported hearing about hauntings and the 1908 murder of Jason Gregory's son-in-law, John Grace.

Ninety years after the end of the Civil War, the United States was in a different kind of struggle—against the rampant unemployment, despair, and poverty of the Depression. Workers from the Civilian Conservation Corps, building Torreya State Park, dismantled the house board by board, ferried it across the river, and reassembled it. The park itself was named for a rare species of the Torreya tree that grows only on the high bluffs above the Apalachicola River, an important steamship transportation route throughout most of the nineteenth century. When the park was built in 1935, it was known as CCC #1 and commemorates the site where, in 1818, then-General Andrew Jackson first crossed the river with his army; later, in 1828, the first government road across northern Florida crossed the river at the site of the park.

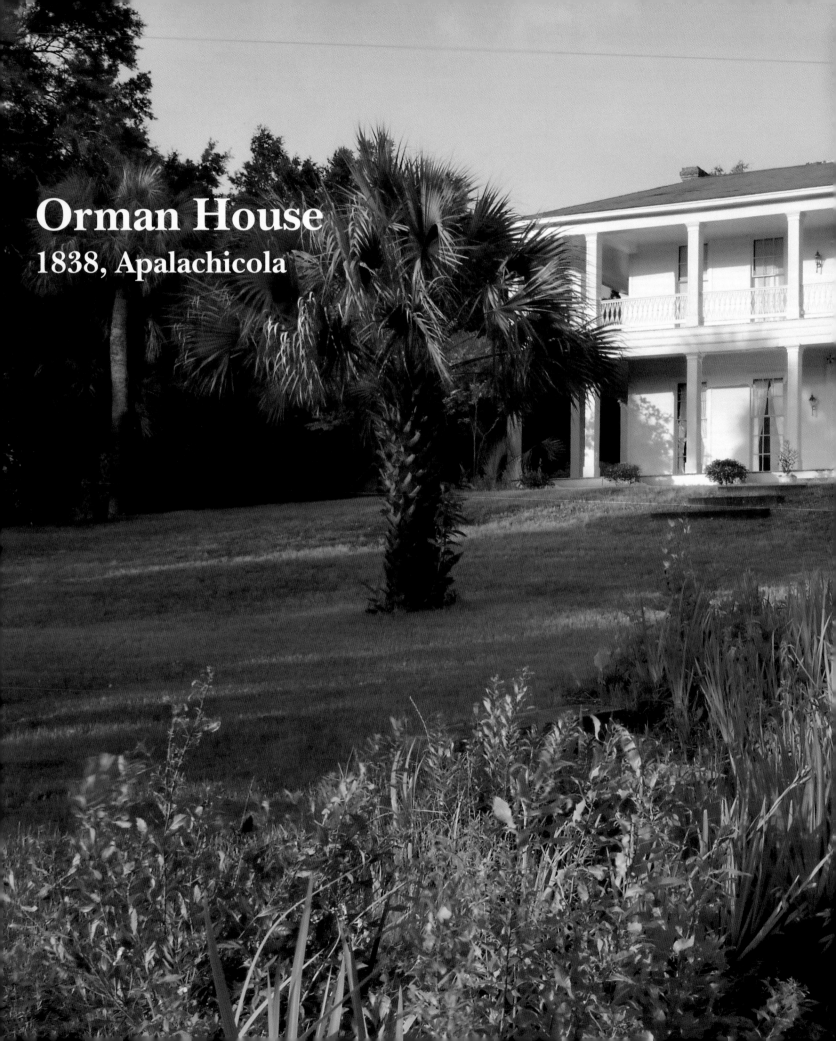

Orman House
1838, Apalachicola

PREVIOUS PAGES
The 1838 home of Thomas Orman stands on a bluff overlooking the Apalachicola River. Orman was a key agent in the success of early Apalachicola as it grew into the third largest cotton-shipping port on the Gulf Coast.

FAR LEFT
The prominent families of Apalachicola entertained extensively in rooms such as the Orman's sumptuous living room. There were European consulates in Apalachicola, and the local families competed for foreign shipping contracts.

NEAR LEFT
At the Ormans's parties, music filled the rooms of the house as guests danced to the melody of Strauss waltzes.

I n the early years of the nineteenth century, the town of Apalachicola flourished as a cotton shipping port. With an abundance of wood milled in northern Florida and the prospect of unending prosperity, wealthy cotton merchants built beautiful and extravagant houses in the elegant architectural styles of the day. Cotton gave way to lumber and lumber to wooden novelty works, and ultimately all gave way to the fishing and oystering industries, but such a litany does not show the vagaries of the economy.

By the last quarter of the twentieth century, Apalachicola's economy had not survived, and with that came the threat to its numerous significant works of architecture. Ultimately, nine hundred properties—ranging from warehouses to grand mansions—within the two-and-a-half- square-mile Apalachicola Historic District were listed on the National Register of Historic Places.

Thomas Orman—a native of the town of Salina, New York, who came to Florida at the age of eighteen—built

such a house, overlooking the Apalachicola River in 1838. Designed with elements of both the prevalent high styles of the era, Federal and Greek Revival, the house was constructed of wood that had been cut to measure in Syracuse, New York, and shipped down the East Coast, around Key West, and up through the Gulf of Mexico. Orman lived there until 1870; his estate included a barn and slave quarters. The house had shutters, broad porches, and six fireplaces. The floors were of wide-plank heart pine, the cornices of molded plaster, and the mantles of wood.

Early images suggest that the house originally had only front porches on both first and second floors and that the porches were later extended around the sides. The house had four rooms at first and was expanded, probably in 1895. It was not many years after that, however, that the house, like so many others in Apalachicola, fell into disrepair. However, in 1994, Annegret and Douglas Gaidry purchased the house and restored it; ultimately in 2000, the Orman House became part of the Florida State Park System.

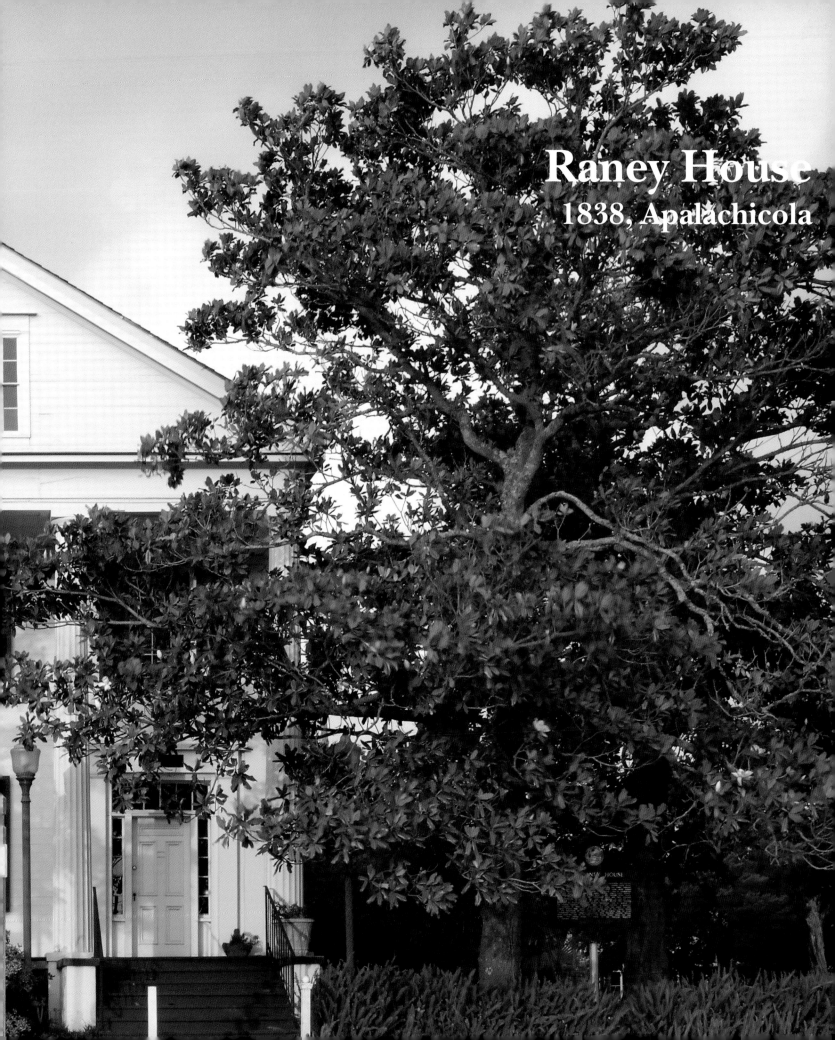

Raney House
1838, Apalachicola

PREVIOUS PAGES
Virginians David Greenway Raney and his wife Harriet built their house several blocks from his cotton-exchange building.

RIGHT
Wide double doors allowed for the family and many guests to move freely from room to room. The dining room table would have been set just before dinner, which was prepared in a kitchen separated from the main house.

I n 1834 David Greenway Raney and Harriet Jordan Raney arrived in Apalachicola from Virginia. David Raney established a commission business and soon began building a bold pedimented house on Market Street; the house, with its four two-story columns, had an imposing presence on the street. Many ships traveled from Apalachicola with cotton and returned with a variety of merchandise, including Aubusson carpets and Italian marble, both used in this house, which was located just blocks from Raney's cotton exchange on Water Street at the Apalachicola River. Raney later became mayor of Apalachicola and was active in civic and social activities.

His family grew to include nine children, six of whom lived into adulthood. When David Raney died in 1881 at age 82, he willed the house to two of his daughters, who in 1914 sold it to Dr. J. S. Murrow. In 1939, the house changed hands again and was turned into a boarding house. The city of Apalachicola purchased it in 1973 and then rented it to the Chamber of Commerce until 1996 when the Apalachicola Area Historical Society purchased and restored it for use as a house museum.

NEAR RIGHT
The late-nineteenth-century Eastlake platform rocker and pump organ are among the many items that have been donated to the Apalachicola Area Historical Society, which maintains the Raney House Museum for the city of Apalachicola.

FAR RIGHT
Heart-pine floors were kept highly buffed by the house servants, whose clothes were made from the fabric woven of the cotton threads made on the spinning wheel. The Raneys ordered their latest fashions from Europe to be shipped on one of the returning vessels.

BELOW
Family rooms upstairs were plainer than downstairs; however, there was a spectacular view of the river. This bedroom could have belonged to the youngest son, George Pettus Raney, who later became chief justice of the State Supreme Court.

Wesley Mansion
1897, Point Washington

PREVIOUS PAGES
*The Wesley House is
surrounded by southern
live oaks, which are
three hundred to five
hundred years old.*

ABOVE AND RIGHT
*The large parlor is
decorated with
eighteenth-century
French provincial
antiques. Among them
are a Louis XVI settee
and chairs purchased in
France, originally from
a chateau (c. 1780).*

I n the mid-1890s William Henry Wesley and
Katie Strickland Wesley built an elegant two-story house
with a double-story wraparound veranda in Point Washington, just miles north of the Gulf of Mexico. At 5,600
square feet, the house was—at that time—the largest in
the region. The Wesley family lived there from 1897
until 1953.

Wesley had bought the land in 1890 to establish a timber business complete with a sawmill, planer mill, and dry
kiln. From a dock at Tucker Bayou, the timber was loaded
onto shallow barges that would then traverse the Chocta-
watchee River to Pensacola where the lumber could be

transferred to larger vessels and head inland or for deep-water transport elsewhere in the United States or to South America or Europe. As was typical in industry in the late nineteenth century, Wesley also built some twenty workers' houses (all now demolished) and continued his lumber operations until shortly after World War I. Remnants of the mill operation, the foundations that did not burn over the years, can still be found on the Eden grounds.

The house was designed in the antebellum style. Katie Strickland Wesley's father, Simeon Strickland, built an identical house nearby, but it has not survived intact. The native yellow-pine wood framing for the house was milled nearby and then floated down the river. The style was typical of houses along the Gulf Coast, up on stilts with rooms placed symmetrically on either side of a central hallway. In the early years, orange trees grew close enough to the house that the family could lean over the railing and pick the fruit.

In 1963, the New York publishing heiress Lois Maxon purchased the house. Maxon renovated and adapted it, removing two original chimneys and adding a new one on the north side as part of her effort to make the house a showplace for her objects and furniture, including one of the largest collections of Louis XVI furniture in America. In 1968, she donated the house and its contents to the state of Florida, after which a reflecting pool was built at the side of the house along with other enhancements.

LEFT
The library originally contained a first-edition collection and is currently decorated with 100- to 180-year-old library furniture. The walnut secretary is from 1830. The portrait is of Joshua Von Smythe, who was Lois Maxon's great grandfather and a furniture maker.

ABOVE
The dining room area is decorated with French and Italian antiques and family heirlooms, including a French mirror from approximately 1810 and an early-nineteenth-century walnut Empire dining table and chairs.

Historic Pensacola Village

Charles Lavalle House
1805

PREVIOUS PAGES
The 1805 Charles Lavalle House is typical of the French Creole cottage-style house with such distinctive architectural elements as the brick nogging on both exterior and interior walls and the beading on the exterior clapboard.

RIGHT
While originally built as a rental property, the Lavalle House eventually became a single-family dwelling, with renovations that included the addition of stairs to the upper garret and interior doorways. Vibrant colors are representative of original paint discovered during architectural investigations.

O n June 11, 1559, Don Tristán de Luna y Arellano set out from Veracruz with an armada of soldiers, colonists, cattle, and horses, expecting to build a town, appoint its government, and provide for its sustenance. Landing at the Bay of Ochuse, he led his troops upriver in search of supplies, while the colonists and remaining soldiers secured the shoreline. Returning one month later, he found that a hurricane had devastated all but three of the ships, destroying both supplies and the community.

In spite of this disastrous foray, historian Irving A. Leonard argues that "a vague belief survived from these early explorations, nevertheless, that somewhere along that mysterious coast was an excellent bay with a great river emptying into it." Whether prompted by the legends of a great port or rumors of French colonization, the Spanish fleet returned in 1698.

Determined to secure the riches of the area and halt French acquisitions coming east from Louisiana, the Spanish established a presidio garrisoned by soldiers, and formalized Spain's claim to Pensacola. When the 1763 Treaty of Paris concluded the Seven Years' War in Europe, Spain ceded Florida to Great Britain, causing the Spanish

George Barkley House
1825

settlers, and the native peoples associated with them, to evacuate to Cuba and other Spanish-held territories.

British opponents of the treaty were not eager to replace them, with early reports claiming Pensacola and Florida to be a "barren swamp." As the first British colony west of the Appalachian Mountains, however, Pensacola attracted Loyalists during the Revolutionary War, and later, settlers motivated by Phineas Lyman's Company of Merchant Adventurers. Although in 1783 Spain reclaimed the land, by 1823, Florida became an American territory.

The houses of Pensacola express the prosperity of the brief British occupation and Pensacola's significance as a center of commerce and trade for the next hundred years. Today, the Historic Pensacola Village includes twenty properties in the Pensacola National Register Historic District, ten of which are open to the public, and four, in particular, reveal the transformation of nineteenth-century Pensacola. The 1805 Charles Lavalle House technically represents Pensacola after its return to Spain, and yet, the architecture is very much related to the British colonial buildings of four-square plans and verandas.

Twenty years later, George Barkley, an English émigré and local entrepreneur in auctioneering, merchandising, and shipping, built the forty-foot-square High